The *Art* of Being a GOOD PARENT

20 Case Studies in Human Development and
the Influence Parents Have on the Mental
and Emotional Health of Their Children

Rosa F. Turner, MD
PSYCHIATRIST

Editing, interior and cover design by ChristianEditingServices.com
Cover art from ShutterStock.com

ISBN 978-0-578-15364-3
Printed in the United States of America

I am dedicating this book to the loving memory of my parents, Rosa Rencurrell de Fernandez and Jose Fernandez Leon, MD.

They had the courage to leave Cuba in 1959, shortly after their country became socialist, despite having a successful dental and medical practice on the island. In search of freedom and democracy, they came to the US with their three daughters, leaving behind their roots and family members as well as the material things they had worked so hard over the years to obtain. Both came from middle-income families, immigrants from France and Spain. They each earned scholarships to study for their careers and they achieved their goals and dreams. As a result of their love, kindness, and understanding, I acquired the strength and courage to work hard and remain happy no matter what obstacles I encounter in life. No words are adequate to describe their lives and tribulations fully.

Thank you, God, for giving them to me, but most of all, thank you, Mom and Dad.

TABLE OF CONTENTS

INTRODUCTION

Most of us understand that our parents raised us as well as they knew how in light of the psychological ideas and principles they believed would help us grow to become healthy, successful, and self-reliant individuals. But professionally developed literature about parenting skills was limited and sparse during most of our parents' lives. Today we are living in a new era. Advances in technology and science have led to a wealth of new information and knowledge in the fields of psychology and psychiatry.

Today we have easy access to an increasing number of books and information on how to be good parents, and along with this there has been an increased awareness of just how important this information is. After all, no one is born knowing how to raise a child. Most people who become parents tend to repeat the patterns and behaviors taught them by their own parents. However, our exposure to and our desire to acquaint ourselves with the growing and developing literature on effective parenting can be of great assistance in helping us break away from the negative patterns we have learned, and embrace the positive as we pursue the important task of becoming better and more effective parents.

It is extremely helpful for people who are considering having children to take a course or seminar or read a book on the subject of effective parenting. Aside from exposing them to good parenting skills, the experience itself may help prospective parents decide whether it is the right time in their lives to become parents. Indeed, some may conclude that the difficult and challenging task of parenthood should be delayed or perhaps even abandoned. Becoming a good parent is not a simple task. Raising our children is one of the most significant experiences in life, and educating ourselves to the challenges involved in that task is vital for both parents and prospective parents.

I wrote this book after completing years of research. I read many books on parenting skills and diagnosed hundreds of innocent children who had become victims of the aggression and ignorance of their parents. Yet there is very little information publicly available to explain *how* parents ought to behave or *why* they should interact with their children in one certain way as opposed to another. In general, I have found that if a person who wishes to do the right thing understands *why* something should be done one way versus another, it begins to make sense to the person, and this makes it more likely he or she will follow through and comply with the recommendations.

I have written this book in the hope that, whether you are a parent or a prospective parent, you will find it informative and helpful in the most important task you will likely ever face in your life—namely, that of parenting and raising a child.

The cases featured in this book are based on actual patients and true events. The names, ages, and background information on the patients discussed in this text have been altered, however, to safeguard confidentiality and to protect the identity of the patients.

Chapter 1

HUMAN DEVELOPMENT

In the early years of life, a child's brain has not yet developed the ability to reason. The brain acts purely on an emotional level. So, for example, a child thinks, "Mommy hit me; so I must be no good." Such a scenario is likely to lead to poor self-esteem, depression, anxiety, and other emotional conflicts and problems, even in the adult years. The more this kind of negative message is reinforced, the greater the chance of an unfortunate outcome during the adolescent and adult years and the greater the probability the conflicts will grow in severity.

Another important facet of early life as humans is that we all have animal instincts. While humans dominate the hierarchy of the animal kingdom, we are also part of it. For example, if a dog growls menacingly at us, we will either flee or get ready to defend ourselves by fighting the aggressor. This instinct is present in the entire animal kingdom, including humans. It is a primitive instinct for preservation of the animal species as a whole.

When a parent hits a child, however, the child is unable to fight back. The child's anger and animal response, however, are still present. It may be temporarily (and sometimes for years) suppressed, but nevertheless it remains within the child as he or she grows older, especially if the parent says to the child, "If you don't stop crying, I'll hit you again," or "Boys don't cry." Crying provides at least a partial release for the child's frustrated anger and humiliation, and if it is not safely permitted, even greater emotional problems typically will develop.

As a child grows older, his or her ability to reason begins to develop; as a result, the child begins to understand why he or she is being hit or otherwise punished. However, this does not change or abolish the suppressed anger the child harbors. This anger may be manifested by depression, anxiety, and other emotional disorders later in life.

If parents are highly abusive, either verbally (for example, calling a child names like "stupid" or "lazy") or physically, the child may feel a sense of instability, which may lead to depression, anxiety, fear, and poor self-esteem. In many instances, it causes the child to develop an inability to make decisions and to experience a sense of malaise and feelings of general failure. The extent of this damage depends on the child's genetic makeup, sensitivity, and environmental factors.

The entire animal kingdom responds best to love and affection (think about your cat purring or your pet dog reveling in being touched by you), and human beings are no different. Affection leads to a sense of well-being and stability: "Mother loves me; therefore I must be good." If consistently experienced, this kind of affection produces a person who is stable and feels good about himself or herself. This is how you want your child to grow up.

Through love and affection you will gain much more and achieve far better results than you will by hitting or screaming at your child. While you will need to discipline your child from time to time, of course, you should always do so in a positive manner; acting in anger and with aggression will lead only to more unruly behavior and compound the problems of unacceptable behavior. Clear demonstrations of your affection and love for your child are extremely important. Saying "I love you" and hugging your child not only helps your child to realize your feelings for him or her are real but also allows your child to feel truly loved and cared for. Reward positive behavior, and discipline your child for negative behavior, but do so in an appropriate way. By doing this, you are providing your child with a sense of stability and self-worth that will carry the child through his or her adolescent and adult years.

There are many ways we can discipline our children. Some are appropriate and very helpful, and some are harmful. Recommended methods include, but are not limited to, *time-out* (requiring the child to cease all activities until the negative energy has dissipated), *taking away privileges* or *depriving the child of objects or experiences* he or she values, *grounding* (not allowing the child to go out with friends or on any type of outing), and the use of *positive and negative reinforcement* in a verbal way (telling your child immediately when you do or do not like something he or she is doing). When your child misbehaves, it is important not to store up your annoyance and express it at a later time. Above all, what children need and most deeply desire is consistency from their parents. All too often, well-intentioned parents end up giving their children mixed messages that serve only to confuse them.

Disciplining methods not recommended include hitting your children, throwing objects in anger, and screaming and yelling at them when they misbehave or make a mistake.

In subsequent chapters I will discuss the different age groups of childhood and address the incentives and disincentives that are most appropriate for each of these age groups. I also will use sample cases to illustrate the significant impact our actions and inactions have on our children. These actions and inactions create a large part of a child's entire environment (family members in the household and their manner of relating to one another, their behaviors, divorce and remarriage in the family, etc.) and have a direct impact on the child's physical well-being, emotional health, sexual wholesomeness, and self-perception.

CASE #1

Mary, a fifteen-year-old adolescent, came to my office accompanied by her mother. Mary sat down across from her mother. She looked sad and kept her eyes focused on the floor. She was short, thin, and pretty, with a mild case of acne on her face.

I interviewed the mother first and then Mary. Her mother said Mary was a quiet, fairly well behaved child until the age of twelve when she became increasingly defiant and angry and frequently argued with her mother. The mother was divorced from Mary's father when Mary was five years old. Mary's mother subsequently remarried when Mary was six years old and had a second child, Robert, who was now nine years of age. The mother was recently separated from her husband, Mary's stepfather, due to marital discord. Mary got along tolerably well with her stepfather but only on a superficial level. She saw her natural father infrequently but reportedly was close to him and missed him. Other symptoms Mary presented on her first visit included poor sleep, poor appetite, low energy, fatigue, low interest, and self-isolating behaviors.

I subsequently interviewed Mary alone. At first, she was highly guarded and answered my questions with only yes or no responses. As time went on, she became more open and began to express herself more freely. She described her mother as a hypocrite, a person who cared more about herself than about Mary or her brother. Mary's voice became increasingly loud with angry undertones as she continued to present her side of the story.

Mary added that her mother frequently would leave her and her brother alone for days, sometimes for a whole week, when she supposedly went on business trips. Mary was in charge of looking after her brother during her mother's prolonged absences. An adult friend of her mother was supposed to be supervising them and coming over every day to check on them, but in reality this happened only rarely. Mary's stepfather seldom visited the house during Mary's mother's absences. He too had a job that required him to leave town frequently.

During our therapy sessions, Mary described herself as feeling sad and empty. She resented her mother for just about everything her mother told her to do or not to do. "She never worried or cared for me; so why should I listen to her?" she said. During my one-on-one sessions with Mary's mother, she said she loved both her children, but she explained that she felt overwhelmed by her job as manager of sales in a large company. Her position required a lot of traveling, and her paycheck barely paid all the bills, including the large mortgage on the home she purchased when she married her second husband.

Mary's mother also explained that she was experiencing a great deal of difficulty obtaining child support from her first husband (Mary's father) or any help with chores such as grocery shopping or keeping up with the house and bills. As she also explained, her job was very stressful and demanding, requiring many hours of overtime for which she was not compensated monetarily. She came home exhausted, just wanting to rest and go to sleep. This took time from her family. She could barely cook a meal for her children. Her weekends were consumed with household chores, cleaning, laundry, and so on. She did not have a social life, for she was too tired to go out with friends on weekends. She had not been involved in a serious relationship after the split with her second husband, and many times she wondered if she would ever meet the right man. She had turned forty recently and felt that life was passing her by.

When I explored Mary's mother's relationship with her children, she admitted she did not have much time for them and said she would frequently be short-tempered and yell at them, especially when she came home from work. She was not very affectionate and was unable to recall the last time she had hugged her kids, kissed them, or said, "I love you." Her own mother and father, Mary's maternal grandparents, had both been cold and distant when Mary's mother was a child, though she said she never thought about it until it came up during the course of our session.

During my sessions with Mary's mother, it became evident she too was suffering from depression and anxiety due to the multiple life stressors in her life. I worked with her to introduce some changes in her life that would benefit both her and her children and hopefully improve the quality of all their lives.

During my early sessions with Mary, the fifteen-year-old said she frequently entertained thoughts of her own death. She wondered what it would be like. She said she felt as if she were no good anyway and no one would ever love her; so what was the use of living? As our early sessions continued, Mary became increasingly angry and irritable, sometimes refusing to attend her session altogether and saying I really did not care for her either. At one point during one of our sessions, she said she wanted to die, and she ran out of my office. I ran after her and brought her back inside. This was one of the turning points in her treatment and therapy.

In this case, the therapeutic process eventually took the form of Mary telling me things she wanted to tell her mother but could not. She would express her anger by yelling and screaming, using me as a target to ventilate her repressed feelings and emotions. The process allowed her to become less irritable, anxious, and depressed. She began developing an improved sense of self-worth and self-esteem and began talking about herself more positively. She became less isolating and more sociable and outgoing, and her depression eventually subsided.

The fact that Mary's mother was receptive to my suggestions and understood my explanations for her daughter's actions helped a great deal in this case. I frequently had sessions together with both of them, and Mary's mother began to gradually improve her ability to express her love and affection for Mary, thereby beginning to provide a corrective experience for her daughter.

Therapy went on for two years on a more or less regular basis. In the beginning I put Mary on an antidepressant, which was eventually discontinued. The case and treatment closed when Mary was seventeen years old. At that time, her affect (the way she carried herself and her ability to hold her head up and meet the eyes of others) was noticeably improved and brighter. She was smiling and going out with friends, and her attitude toward life had changed significantly. Her grades improved in school, her voice was of a more normal tone, and she no longer screamed and yelled in frustration. She was communicating with her mother much more richly, and the entire family of three was getting along much better.

Two years later I received a call from Mary. She had finished high school with honors and was in her first year of college. She indicated that she wanted to be a teacher for emotionally handicapped children. She had a boyfriend, and she was enjoying college and doing well in her classes. I never heard from her again, but I feel confident her life had been greatly improved by my attentive and concerned listening and by my interventions during her therapy.

The fact that Mary's mother was intelligent and cooperative was very important to the success of the treatment. Unfortunately, many therapy cases do not have as good an outcome. Mary's case illustrates a number of key issues in child development. Essentially, Mary had been ignored and deprived of love and affection by her parents, and this contributed to poor self-esteem and feelings of anger and frustration.

As noted earlier, a child's sense of well-being and security is influenced enormously by love, attention, and the positive feedback he or she receives from parents, especially during the early developmental years. Mary's mother was unaware of the impact her actions were having on her daughter. Thankfully, she had not been physically abusive toward Mary. The more severe and/or frequent the abuse experienced by a child, the more difficult and challenging therapy becomes. In some instances, the abuse and damage directed against a child is so severe it is simply too late to effect positive therapeutic changes.

Many factors played a role in the success of Mary's treatment. Mary was very intelligent and had a strong genetic composition. This, along with her mother's ability to understand and cooperate with treatment directives, facilitated a positive outcome to the treatment.

Another important point illustrated by Mary's case is that the earlier the therapeutic intervention occurs, the higher the rate of success. This is because development is still occurring. It is during the early phase of adolescence that children typically develop their ability to reason and understand. At the same time, they are also young enough to change certain patterns of behavior through treatment. It is much more difficult to effect change in the case of adults, as they have already formed basic behavioral characteristics and patterns of behavior. Research and clinical experience show that the older one becomes, the more set one's characterological structure becomes.

Mary's is just one of many cases I will be sharing with you throughout this book, in order to introduce and highlight key and important points for effective parenting.

CASE #2

Five-year-old Tommy was brought to my office by his foster mother. Tommy was a slim and very cute little boy with blond hair and big blue eyes. He quietly sat down next to his foster mother with his head down.

I began by asking Tommy some simple questions, trying to engage him in conversation. Gradually, he began to look up at me more frequently, but he did not smile. He acted shy and looked sad most of the time. He appeared nervous and at times was fidgety. According to his foster mother, Tommy was a picky eater, but he managed to stay within the normal height/weight ratio for his age. He was sleeping satisfactorily, but he would move around in bed during his sleep and sometimes wake up with nightmares, screaming. Tommy said he felt very scared at those times, thinking monsters were coming after him. As I continued my evaluation, there was no evidence of psychotic symptoms and no presence of auditory or visual hallucinations or paranoia. The child's thought process was appropriate and coherent.

The reason his foster mother brought Tommy to me was his aggressive and defiant behavior at home and at school. She was receiving frequent notes and phone calls from the child's very concerned kindergarten teacher. He was not paying attention at school and frequently got up from his seat. He was now becoming more disruptive and defiant in class. This was happening at least once or twice per week. He was very quiet at times but had a very low frustration tolerance. There were frequent angry outbursts both at home and at school. He got along only with a few of his peers but, again, was easily agitated when he did not get what he wanted. He had developed the habit of taking things from his peers and disrupting the entire activity in which the class was engaged.

At home Tommy's behavior was similar. He showed no respect for authority figures. When his mother told him to stop doing something, he refused or simply said, "No!" in a very aggressive, angry voice.

There was no known family history of psychiatric illness. Tommy recently had had a complete medical checkup and the workup, including an MRI of the brain, was normal. The only noteworthy medical observations were old bruises and scars on his legs and his upper and lower back.

Tommy was living with his foster mother, her husband, and their fourteen-year-old daughter and seven-year-old son. Tommy had been removed from his biological mother by legal authorities at the age of three and a half because of severe neglect and physical abuse. His biological mother frequently went out with boyfriends and did not adequately care for her son. According to reports from investigations, his natural mother frequently would scream and yell at her boy. He also was subjected to severe corporal punishment, as his mother frequently hit him with brooms, extension cords, wood paddles, and sticks. At times she would lock Tommy up in his room when she had friends visiting. Tommy never saw his biological father, as he left the house soon after Tommy was born. Tommy had no biological siblings.

Prior to his current placement, Tommy had spent several months in a shelter. His foster mother and father, Mr. and Mrs. Thompson, accepted him as their foster child, hoping eventually to be able to adopt him. Tommy had been with them for approximately a year. When he first came to live with them, he was very quiet and stayed alone in a room he shared with Andy, the Thompsons' son.

Mr. Thompson was the president of a large construction company in the South Florida area. Mrs. Thompson was a housewife. They were a very religious family and attended church every Sunday. They had always wanted a large family, but Mrs. Thompson was unable to have any more children after her daughter and son were born. The

Thompsons were a warm and loving couple who did not believe in corporal punishment and were appalled when they heard about the cruel behavior that had been directed against Tommy. Their own two children were doing well in school and at home, and there had never been any complaints from school about bad behavior. On the contrary, their academic achievements and grades were exemplary, and they conducted themselves appropriately in the classroom.

As time progressed, Tommy and Andy began arguing and fighting, and the situation grew progressively worse. Tommy became increasingly angry and very irritable, and he always blamed Andy for the discord between them. The Thompsons tried several methods of discipline, including time-out and taking away privileges, and they treated the two boys equally when they did not know who started a fight. However, Tommy became more and more defiant and disobedient anyway, and on occasion he would leave the house and slam the door. It was at this point the Thompsons decided to seek psychiatric help. They did not know what to do, but instead of giving up on Tommy they decided to seek professional help and advice.

After my initial evaluation of Tommy, I recommended intensive individual psychotherapy with medication to help modulate his behavior. At Tommy's age, therapy is usually conducted in the form of play therapy, whereby through the use of different objects in the playroom the child is able to release his repressed anger by reliving his experiences and releasing the built-up emotions of his early, traumatic years. A young child's brain has not yet developed the capacity to reason and rationalize; this begins in late childhood and early adolescence. As a result, a child is unable to verbalize his feelings the way adults can. Play therapy provides a medium for the expression of these feelings in young children and the release of the emotions connected to the traumatic events in their lives.

We began the play therapy sessions by creating a house with a family living in it. Together we picked a mother, a father, and one child. As therapy progressed, Tommy's play became increasingly more aggressive. He picked up the mother figure and began hitting the child and beating it against the ground with the mother figure. He would yell and scream and at times cry while doing this. These sessions continued with the same theme surfacing again and again, and they became increasingly more intense as his anger grew. The father figure was thrown across the room and against the wall. I allowed him to play with the figures as he wished, intervening at times to make therapeutic comments designed to help him release his anger.

After six months, Tommy's anger slowly began to subside. I also began to work with the Thompsons to help Tommy at home and explained what was happening and how to handle difficult situations with him. After approximately one year, Tommy had made significant progress, and with the help of a behavior modification program and medication he was able to make significant changes in school and at home. I recommended a treatment plan for another year to increase his chances of success. Eventually, the Thompsons agreed to adopt Tommy, and he was legally adopted at the age of eight. Therapy continued but at significantly less frequency and intensity, and in time the medications were discontinued.

Every case is multifactorial. Many cases like Tommy's fall through the cracks due to inadequate funds for such intense therapy or the unavailability or unwillingness of parents to go through the process and be as cooperative and supportive as the Thompsons were. Tommy was very lucky to have had the opportunity to enter into and experience intensive therapy.

This case offers a perfect example of the impact physical abuse has on a child. Tommy's extreme anger, aggression, and defiance were primarily consequences of the severe physical abuse and neglect he had been subjected to while living with his biological mother. Fortunately, he was removed from that environment at the relatively young age of three and a half, with his young brain being highly receptive and open to therapeutic intervention. In general, the younger the person is when corrective action is taken, the better will be the outcome.

This case also highlights the importance of a loving environment. The Thompsons were loving and demonstrative in their love, and this provided a positive corrective experience for Tommy, who was young enough to be able to gain from its positive effects. Five years later Tommy is still living with the Thompsons and is doing well.

PARENTING PRINCIPALS TO REMEMBER:

> Never hit or scream at your child.
> Avoid giving your child negative messages; never call your child names.
> Clearly demonstrate love and affection for your child.
> Discipline for negative behavior, but also remember to reward positive behavior.
> Be consistent!

Chapter 2

INFANCY AND CHILDHOOD

(AGES ZERO - TWELVE)

INFANCY (AGES ZERO–TWO)

These are referred to as the "formative" years because it is during this time span that the basis and foundation for a child's proper development are formed. Young children react on an emotional level. The ability to reason begins to develop only late in this stage and improves with age. At that point you are able to speak to a child and explain that his or her behavior is unacceptable. The child gradually begins to understand you and is able to respond in a more appropriate way. It is also during this period that consequences for behavior may be explained to the child. Rules must be consistently enforced. Otherwise, the child learns he or she may get away with thing some times and not at others. The result is that the behavior is not abolished. Again, consistency is the key to your interaction with your child and crucial in facilitating positive changes.

Never say, "You are a bad boy/girl." (Children who hear such statements begin to believe them, and this leads to problems later in life.) Instead, tell your child that what he or she is doing is not correct, and explain why he or she is being punished. Also, set ground rules and consequences ahead of time so that the child knows what to expect. Giving the child a prior warning helps to decrease the chances of angry and emotional outbursts.

Very few children are taken for psychiatric evaluations during this age span, for obvious reasons. This is, however, a critical time in the life of every child. An excerpt from *The Comprehensive Textbook of Psychiatry*, citing a couple of studies bearing on this period, illustrates just how critical this early stage of life is:

Bowlby, in 1952, on the basis of an extensive review of the literature available at the time, concluded that early separation and emotional deprivation had persistent and irreversible effects on personality traits and behavior. Bowlby's studies on maternal deprivation served to call attention to the disastrous and far-reaching effects of early neglect.

Goldfarb compared the behavior in adolescence of two groups of children abandoned in infancy. The [members of the] first group remained in an orphanage for the first three years of their lives and then were placed in foster care; the second group of children were placed in foster care early in infancy. The foster homes for the two groups were said to be substantially alike. As adolescents, the children institutionalized for the first three years showed lower IQ's, inferior school performance and sociopathic traits.[1]

We have all heard of the "terrible twos." This really is a difficult phase of early childhood development, and it is made more difficult by parents who wrongly assume their children can understand them at this point and purposely are disobeying in order to aggravate them. Yet this is clearly not the case. This is an age when a parent needs to be particularly tolerant of the child's behavior because it will not be

---

1   Alfred M. Freedman and Harold L. Kaplan, eds., *The Comprehensive Textbook of Psychiatry* (Baltimore: Williams & Wilkins, 1967), 1323, 1324.

possible to control every important aspect of that behavior. At this age, for example, children frequently have temper tantrums for no apparent reason. The best way to discourage such behavior is to ignore it for a few minutes and then pick up the child and hug him or her and be supportive. Children at this age need attention, and if they are unable to get it in a positive way they will seek it through negative and "acting-out" behaviors.

This is also the age of curiosity. You will see children at this stage taking pots and pans out of kitchen cabinets and running around the house messing things up for no apparent reason. You may have to adjust to this mess and ignore it. (It is not a lasting phase—that is the good news.)

Remember that if you hit a child who is already crying, he or she will cry more and louder, aggravating you even more. So with a child at this age, you need to be very tolerant and very loving. This requires a lot of patience; so begin to practice patience now if you plan on having and raising children.

There is still much to be learned about this period of development, but its significance cannot be overlooked.

EARLY CHILDHOOD (AGES THREE–SEVEN)

As we move along from age two into early childhood, we find that a child responds best to positive reinforcement and love. If one takes something (for example, a toy) away from a child, the child will cry in protest. It then becomes the parent's job, gently and lovingly, to discourage this behavior for the future since it is universally aggravating or disturbing to parents when their children scream and yell. So instead of taking something away from a child abruptly, try diverting his or her attention to something else and substituting one object the child likes for another. Be creative. At this age, do not expect a child to understand why he or she should not be playing with something that might be harmful. Many parents assume their children think like adults, and they expect their children to behave simply because they must "do what they are told." This is clearly not the case!

You may begin to speak to a child between the ages of three and seven and attempt to explain the difference between good and bad and right and wrong. You may also use various types of punishments and negative incentives. These may include time-out or having the child stand in a corner for five to ten minutes (five minutes at ages three to four, and up to ten minutes between the ages of five and seven). At this point you should explain to the child what he or she did and why it is wrong. It is OK to say to the child, "Whenever you do something that is not right (do not use the word or the concept of "bad" because the child will generalize and internalize it), I have to punish you." Hug your child and put him or her in a corner facing the wall. Always follow through with what you say you are going to do, otherwise your child will not take your words seriously. You must be consistent or your child will quickly learn that he or she sometimes can get away with unacceptable behavior. It is also important that there be agreement between parents that one parent does not reduce or cancel the punishment another parent has introduced or established.

Remember, do not yell or scream at your child. Interventions work best when you are cool, calm, and collected, and are consistent. Demonstrate to the child that you are in control (this also will help him or her to be in control), and carry out the punishment without hesitation and feelings of guilt.

CASE #3

Vanessa, a striking blond-haired, blue-eyed four-year-old, was brought to my office for severe emotional problems. She was very anxious and hyperactive and physically aggressive toward her peers with biting and kicking behaviors. She also exhibited sexual acting-out behavior.

Vanessa's foster mother, with whom the child had been living for approximately two months, said that during the prior year Vanessa had been in multiple foster homes because her behavior had been unruly and uncontrollable. Her disruptive behavior in each of the different foster environments eventually led to removal and placement in another foster home.

Vanessa was born in North Carolina to Mr. and Mrs. Brown. She had lived with them for three years before being removed to foster care. Her biological parents moved to South Florida when Vanessa was two years old. Her father worked as a truck driver and her mother was a housewife. I never had the opportunity to interview Vanessa's biological parents as their parental rights had been terminated by the courts. From records and the account of Vanessa's current foster mother, however, I learned the following: Her father had lost his job on multiple occasions. At some point he had become a crack cocaine abuser and sold drugs on the streets. The mother also became an abuser. To our knowledge, however, Vanessa had never been directly exposed to drug abuse.

Vanessa's childhood situation came to the attention of the Florida Department of Children and Families because of reports from Mrs. Allen, the mother of Vanessa's playmate, a little girl about the same age as Vanessa, who lived next door. During the children's play sessions, it became evident to Mrs. Allen that Vanessa was playing in a sexually provocative manner. At one point she heard Vanessa tell her daughter, "Let's take off our clothes and play." At that point Mrs. Allen stopped the behavior and redirected the children to a different activity.

Vanessa frequently would stay overnight at her neighbor's house. On these occasions Mrs. Allen took good care of Vanessa and fed her. However, many times Vanessa would sleep over at Mrs. Allen's house because her own parents had failed to pick her up; and as this neglectful behavior on the part of Vanessa's parents became more frequent, Mrs. Allen began to worry.

Another reason for concern in this case was that when Vanessa was at home with her parents, Mrs. Allen frequently would hear the child screaming and yelling. Mrs. Allen eventually brought her concerns to the attention of the police department when the screaming and yelling on one occasion continued on for an entire hour. The police subsequently searched Vanessa's home and found drug paraphernalia and signs of parental neglect. Vanessa's room was dirty, her sheets looked as if they had not been washed for some time, and there were roaches amid her scattered toys. In short, the place was a mess.

After the search, Vanessa and her three-month-old baby brother were physically removed from their home and placed in foster care. Reports of the investigation later indicated that Vanessa had been the victim of frequent physical and emotional abuse. Vanessa had been exposed to sexual behavior as well, watching as her parents removed their clothes and engaged in sexually intimate behavior. There also was evidence that Vanessa was present when pornographic movies were being viewed in the home. Vanessa unquestionably had been hit with a belt and with an extension cord. This physical abuse occurred especially when her father was using drugs. Her mother was also abusive physically. Vanessa had no further contact with her parents subsequent to her removal from their home.

Vanessa initially was placed in a foster home where the foster parents were warm and loving. However, there were two other foster children in the same home and Vanessa quickly became a problem. She would instigate fights and arguments, and it became very difficult for her foster parents to control her behavior. As a result, Vanessa was placed in another foster home and then another. Unfortunately (but not unexpectedly), her behavior worsened and she became completely uncontrollable. At that point, her current foster mother brought her to my office.

As of this writing, Vanessa has been in therapy for several months and is slowly making progress. Her current foster mother appears to be a very organized and competent individual. She has three other foster children and is supportive and cooperative with therapy and Vanessa's treatment. So far, the clinical interventions have been successful and Vanessa hopefully will be able to remain in this foster home.

This very sad case is a direct and predictable result of bad parenting skills that led to instability and complete chaos in Vanessa's early childhood years. Her parents were deeply out of control in terms of their own behavior, and their child was subjected to severe emotional and physical abuse. This case clearly demonstrates how the underlying sadness of the child, due to lack of affection and physical abuse, manifested itself in the form of anger and aggressive play. Vanessa's anxiety was evident from her extreme hyperactivity. She also began acting out sexually due to having been exposed to sexual acts. As a child, she was confused about what she was being exposed to. As we shall see in subsequent cases, children are frequently exposed to sexual activity in our society with severe repercussions. In many cases, these children are not provided with corrective therapy at an early age and they simply "fall through the cracks." Later, in late adolescence and adulthood, this early childhood abuse frequently leads to sociopathic behavior and acts of physical and sexual violence.

CASE #4

Henry, a cute little six-year-old, brown-haired, brown-eyed boy, was brought to my office for treatment by his mother, Mrs. Garcia. Henry was being defiant in school, frequently getting into fights, and behaving disruptively in class. Henry's mother reported that he was defiant at home as well, frequently hitting his three-year-old half sister and yelling and screaming at his parents whenever he was disciplined. He was particularly hostile toward his mother, who said, "The more I hit him, the worse he gets. I don't understand him."

Mrs. Garcia divorced Henry's dad when Henry was just two years old. They had resided as a family in Miami-Dade County, but after the divorce Mr. Garcia left Miami and went back to his native Puerto Rico. Henry had not seen his biological dad since. When Henry was three years old, his mother married Mr. Miller, who appears to be a caring individual.

I interviewed Mr. Miller, Henry's stepfather, separately from his wife. Mr. Miller said his wife physically hit her son frequently; he had tried to discourage this behavior on her part but, as he explained, she did not appear to think it was a problem. He reported that his wife's attitude worsened after their daughter was born. Henry's mother was overwhelmed with having a newborn and also dealing with Henry. Despite her happiness at having given birth to a girl, she clearly took out her frustrations on Henry without realizing it.

I spoke with Henry, but he was shy and very soft-spoken. He told me he had nightmares and sometimes woke up at night thinking monsters were out to get him. He appeared nervous when I asked about his fighting at school. He said he could not help it because other kids were making fun of him or picking on him; so he hit them. I asked Henry about his parents, and he said he really got along with his "dad" (stepfather) and liked him a lot; he said he loved his mother too, but she made him mad. "She is always screaming and yelling at me and hits me with a belt. I think she loves my sister more than me."

I recommended individual and family therapy for Henry and his family. I also spoke to Mrs. Garcia privately and referred her to parenting classes.

Henry's case allows us to see the importance of emotional development during the early childhood years. In spite of the later corrective experience his stepfather had been providing for the child for approximately a year, and despite his mother's improvement in parenting methods as a result of her parenting classes, Henry continued to manifest aggressive behavior toward his younger sister, whom his mother clearly did favor, perhaps because Henry unconsciously reminded her of the husband who had abandoned her. (Even at this age, children experience sibling rivalry.) After several months of therapy, however, progress became evident. Henry's behavior in school improved, and his relationship with his mother became closer and more trusting. Therapy was suggested until all issues were resolved. The fact that this intervention was started at a very young age will have a large, positive impact on the outcome.

Henry's mother's willingness to change is also of major significance in this case. Mrs. Garcia was willing to take parenting classes, and her desire to identify and understand her mistakes were crucial components in helping the situation improve as the therapy progressed. She made positive changes in her parenting skills and was able to become emotionally closer to her son as a result of her corrections.

CASE #5

Andrew, a seven-year-old, brown-haired, hazel-eyed, thin, tall, and handsome boy, was brought to my office by his paternal grandmother, Anne Harrison. Mrs. Harrison brought Andrew to me at the request of his school counselor. Andrew was exhibiting disruptive behaviors and defiance in school and at home. He also had temper tantrums and frequently broke out crying over seemingly small things. Andrew habitually fought with his siblings and argued with and talked back to his grandmother. Mrs. Harrison reported that Andrew's behavior problems began soon after he was separated from his biological parents at the age of five, and since then they had become progressively worse.

Unlike many other traumatized children, Andrew was able to verbalize his feelings of sadness and anger. He told me he became sad and cried at times when he thought about his parents, and he expressed how much he missed them, especially his mother, to whom he had been very close. He remembered his father hitting his mother with his fists and throwing her around the room. His mother would throw objects back at her husband in response. Scenes like these occurred very frequently, the boy said. On several occasions the neighbors called the police, until finally the children were removed from the home. They were first taken to a shelter and finally to live with their grandmother. Parental rights were terminated and Andrew had not seen his parents since the separation.

Andrew's parents fought with each other, but they never hit him or his brother and sister. Andrew explained that it was very painful to see these fights, but not seeing his parents at all was even worse. He missed his parents and was very angry at not being able to see them. At first he had hopes of the whole family being together again someday, but now he was not sure he would ever see his parents again. This was very frustrating for him. He had nightmares and often wondered whether his parents were all right.

Andrew was currently living with his grandmother, his nine-year-old brother, and his six-year-old sister. They had aunts, uncles, and cousins, but these relatives lived far away and were not in close contact with Andrew. He also worried about his grandmother, whose health was not good, and wondered who would take care of him and his siblings if something happened to her. He was able to explain that her illnesses made him sad because he loved her a lot.

I referred Andrew for both individual psychotherapy and family therapy to help him ventilate his feelings of anger, frustration, and sadness and to help improve the quality of his family life and relationships and patterns of communications between family members.

This case exemplifies the significant impact parents have on their children, their development, and their behavior. It demonstrates the importance of parental love and affection, the absence of which leads to sadness, depression, and anxiety. It also brings out the significance of the different inborn traits children exhibit. As the most sensitive of the three siblings, Andrew was the one most affected by the absence of the parents and by the anxiety over the possible loss of a loved one (his grandmother), especially at such a young age.

LATE CHILDHOOD (AGES EIGHT–TWELVE)

At ages eight to twelve, the child's brain has developed more and is able to recognize the rationale for punishment and the difference between right and wrong. Now, instead of five to ten minutes of time-out, you might consider taking away your child's privileges, such as watching television or a favorite television program, playing Nintendo, or being with friends. It is very important, however, that you not take privileges away for a long time. In this age group (depending on the severity of the act and its frequency), removal of privileges generally should not be for longer than one evening. Also, you can use positive reinforcement. For example, you can give your child an opportunity to do something especially desirable this weekend if he or she does well in school, or has his or her room cleaned up by Friday, or if there are no negative reports of behavior sent home from school. These methods can vary depending on what the problem is. Most important of all, always remember to be consistent and to remain cool and under control in your interactions with your child.

CASE #6

Laura, a shy, pretty eight-year-old with beautiful eyes and long black hair, was brought to my office by her mother after the girl had touched two boys at school inappropriately on their behinds, backs, and knees. The first incident occurred several months earlier, and the second one just the day before I saw Laura. Laura said she heard a voice inside her head telling her to do things like this and explained that she did them without thinking. Other symptoms she exhibited were anxiety and sadness to the point of crying when she thought of her cousin (more about this below). She also became very nervous at times for no apparent reason.

Laura currently was living with her mother, stepfather, and two-year-old half sister. Her parents were divorced four years earlier, when she was four years old. Laura was very close to her father and she saw him occasionally on weekends. She got along well with her stepfather and said he was nice to her. Laura loved her mother, who appeared to be a warm and caring individual.

After her parents' divorce, Laura spent a lot of time at her nearby aunt's house. She played with her cousins and frequently spent the night at her cousins' house. During this period, she was sexually molested by her twenty-one-year-old cousin. The abuse went on for about one year. She did not tell her mother because her cousin told her not to do so, and Laura was afraid of him. She finally told her mother because "she couldn't take it anymore." Apparently, the abuse included penetration in Laura's rectum but not her vagina. Her cousin later served time in prison for his behavior. Laura was never allowed to stay at her aunt's house after the discovery of this sexual abuse, but her younger cousins were allowed to come and play at her house.

When she was six, Laura had gone to therapy for severe anxiety, fears, and nightmares. Her therapist diagnosed her as suffering from post-traumatic stress syndrome with nervousness and fear being the result. When Laura came to see me, she was still suffering from anxiety and depressive symptoms. Her parents also had been arguing a lot and she feared they might separate.

I referred Laura for further individual and family therapy. In spite of her having received therapy in the past, symptom resolution for the traumatic episodes of sexual abuse had not occurred. She was confused about what had happened between her and her cousin and why it had occurred. She found it difficult to keep herself from touching the boys at her school inappropriately and did not understand why she did it. She obviously needed more therapy for ventilation of symptoms and to help her better control her inappropriate and symptomatic behavior. Laura also needed to work on her anxiety over possible parental separation, which is often a severe stressor for small children. This was particularly true in the case of Laura, who already had been through this experience before.

This case highlights some very important factors in childhood development and appropriate parenting. Laura received love from her parents, and there was no physical abuse; so at least these important factors were on the positive side of the ledger in her development. Her anxiety regarding parental separation, though, demonstrates the important role marital stability plays in childhood development. In order to feel safe and secure and to grow up to be stable and free of anxiety-related disorders as an adult, a child needs parents who have a solid relationship. As we see from case after case, parental separation, which many parents would prefer to think does not impact their children, is always a crucial and traumatic event for a child. Unfortunately, divorce and the breakup of relationships are all too common in our society. This is why parents need to understand that they must do everything reasonably possible to make the transition smooth and less traumatic for their children and to try, as much as possible, to insure their children are not victimized and wounded by the process of a divorce.

Finally, we see the potentially enormous impact sexual abuse has on children, especially when perpetrated on young children, whose personalities are being formed. They easily become confused and traumatized, as they lack the capacity to understand that what is being done to them is not their fault. Laura was fortunate that her mother believed her when she related the story of her cousin's sexual behavior toward her. Parents often do not believe their child, especially when the abuser is a spouse or a close family member. The failure on the part of parents to believe an account of sexual abuse can be catastrophic. It typically contributes to the abuse continuing, further traumatizing the child. When a child's report of abuse is denied or not taken seriously, the child is, in effect, being victimized a second time. The dismissal severely affects the victim's career, social relationships, and feelings of self-esteem.

Laura was very fortunate to receive therapy. Sexual abuse in childhood is more frequent than most people imagine. The worst thing about unrecognized and untreated sexual abuse in childhood, however, is that many children do not receive help and become future perpetrators, abusing other children, ending up in jail, or worse.

CASE #7

Lilly was a brown-haired, brown-eyed, slightly overweight ten-year-old. Her grandmother brought her to my office. Lilly had had behavior problems since she was five years old, and they had gradually worsened. She was very manipulative and lost her temper easily when she did not get what she wanted. According to her grandmother, Mrs. Freeman, Lilly became angry and had poor impulse control. She also became sad and broke down in tears for no apparent reason.

Lilly currently was living with her grandmother, her aunt, two young cousins, and her stepgrandfather. She had a nineteen-year-old brother who lived in New York, but she rarely saw him. Her mother lived in Miami and visited her occasionally. Her father was killed in an automobile accident when Lilly was two years old, and she did not remember him consciously but she wished he were alive. She had lived with her mother until she was five years old. Due to her mother having two jobs and an active social life, however, Lilly was frequently left in the care of her grandmother until she finally came to live with her.

Lilly said she missed living with her mother because she could do whatever she wanted to during her mother's absences from home. Her stepgrandfather was very strict and occasionally hit her when her grandmother was not around. Lilly blamed her grandmother for not letting her see her mother. (In reality, her mother just did not come to see her, and her grandmother made excuses.) She said her grandmother was very nice to her and gave her whatever she wanted. She always got her way, especially when she cried, screamed, or threw a temper tantrum. However, while this worked at home, it did not work so well at school.

Lilly's grandmother had been getting more and more calls from school about her granddaughter's behavior. Lilly had frequently been getting into arguments with her peers and talking back to teachers. She also had begun skipping classes. Her grades had deteriorated, and she was now failing fifth grade. Mrs. Freeman said she could not take it anymore. She said she had always treated Lilly well and had felt sorry for her due to her "circumstances." She saw Lilly cry sometimes when she was alone, and this broke her heart.

I referred Lilly for individual and family therapy. I also referred her grandmother and stepgrandfather to parenting classes, which they agreed to attend.

This case involves several important stressors that deeply affect children. Lilly's father died when she was two. Although she does not remember him, she wishes he were alive. It is a biological instinct to want to have our parents with us. Psychologically, this loss of a parent is translated and felt in the child's mind, at a primitive, instinctual level, as a form of abandonment. Lilly also missed her mother, who in a real sense did abandon her. Lack of parental love, nurture, and stability often leads to depressive and anxiety disorders later in life, depending on other circumstances. Lilly already was exhibiting signs of sadness, frustration, and anger, which are manifestations of underlying depression.

Lilly's stepgrandfather hit her on occasion but was not severely abusive. Her grandmother was the one person who demonstrated love and affection toward her and was a very positive force in her life. A child needs to be loved (acknowledged) by at least one significant person in life in order to establish an identity and feel worthy and secure.

Here again we see the effect of poor parenting skills. The child in this case was allowed to do whatever she wanted, without structure or boundaries. As a result, she had learned to become manipulative in order to get her way. Her manipulative techniques and behavior, however, did not pay off outside her home, and she suffered the consequences at school in relationships with her peers and teachers. We do not always get what we want in life just because we want it.

CASE #8

Angelo, a tall, slim, brown-haired, green-eyed twelve-year-old, was brought to my office by his mother, Mrs. Johnston. Angelo suffered from angry outbursts. He felt sad and depressed and cried often. He was not very sociable and isolated himself. As a result, he had few friends. His symptoms had been present since he was eight years old but had gradually worsened over the intervening four years. For the past few months, he had been telling his mother he sometimes felt like jumping out of the car while it was moving. He also reported that he had tried to choke himself with a rope but suddenly stopped. He wondered what dying would be like. Understandably, Angelo's mother became concerned about his statements and made an emergency appointment with me.

Angelo lived with his mother, his stepfather, and a younger half brother who was four years old. His parents were divorced when he was six years old. They argued and fought constantly. Angelo saw his father hitting his mother and felt helpless. He would try to stop his father from abusing his mother but ended up getting thrown out of the way. He was also the victim of severe physical and emotional abuse by his dad. His father would routinely pull down Angelo's pants and hit him hard with a wooden board on his behind. The more Angelo cried, the harder he was hit. This happened often, and Angelo said he had never forgotten how badly it hurt. He sometimes felt his father did not love him and never had. Angelo had not seen his father very often after the divorce, but he wanted to see him. Angelo frequently wondered where his father was and what he might be doing. His mother had been good to him, and he knew she loved him unconditionally.

Ever since Angelo's younger half brother was born, though, Angelo felt his mother had changed. Angelo always was blamed and ended up being punished whenever there was a fight between the siblings. His younger brother went into Angelo's room and took whatever he wished. He sometimes broke Angelo's things, but no one punished him for it. Angelo had now concluded that his mother loved his brother more than she loved him. He got along with his stepdad, but the relationship was not very close. He sometimes felt as if he were the black sheep of the family.

I referred Angelo for individual psychotherapy to help him understand, cope with, and ventilate his feelings. I also prescribed family therapy to counter the negative environmental and family influences that were stressing Angelo and having such a negative impact on him.

Angelo was a victim of multiple, severe traumatic events in his life. He witnessed domestic violence that he was helpless to stop, and he was subjected to severe physical and emotional abuse by his biological father. In spite of this, he wanted to see and become closer to his father (still looking for his approval and love). Later, after the birth of his half brother, Angelo's mother neglected him and clearly gave the lion's share of her positive attention and love to her younger child. This caused Angelo to respond with attention-seeking behavior in school, where he had become increasingly defiant and rebellious.

The cumulative impact of the neglect, abuse, and lack of nurture gradually triggered Angelo's depressive symptoms. He had poor self-esteem, which had led to his social isolation and lack of friends. He did not feel worthy of having friends because he was used to feeling worthless as a consequence of the neglect and abuse he had been subjected to most of his life. His depression had progressed to the point that he cried often and had recently been having thoughts of dying. Life appeared to have no purpose. The meaning of joy and happiness was not familiar to Angelo. He was a sensitive child, which made the impact even worse. He was lucky to have the chance to receive the individual and family help he needed.

As I have previously noted, depression is usually manifested in the form of anger. This anger can be, and often is, turned inward against oneself. Those who internalize their anger in this way tend to be withdrawn and isolated and, if left untreated, might eventually commit suicide. Individuals who turn their anger outward are usually the ones we see screaming and yelling. They often end up harming others rather than themselves.

PARENTING PRINCIPALS TO REMEMBER:

> Explain to your child why certain behaviors are unacceptable and what the consequences of them are.

> Explain the difference between right and wrong.

> Enforce rules consistently.

> Give your child the attention he or she needs.

> Be patient!

> Provide the marital stability orderliness, structure, and boundaries children need.

> Protect your child from exposure to sexual activity and materials.

> Do not dismiss reports of physical or sexual abuse.

> Be careful never to favor one child over another.

Chapter 3

ADOLESCENCE

(AGES THIRTEEN-EIGHTEEN)

Many have said the adolescent years are the most difficult in a person's life. The child is growing and slowly becoming an adult. His or her ability to understand and reason has developed and is now being fine-tuned.

This period can be a very emotionally trying and even a horrible experience for both children and their parents. There are many different and new problems the child faces as he or she goes out into the world to meet its challenges. The adolescent child now has the task of making friends, adjusting to high school, and facing social pressures often not understood by parents. The pressures we parents faced during our adolescence are very different from the pressures adolescents today face. We tend to expect our children to do what we did at the same age, but this is seldom possible because the world and the people in it have changed during the past decades.

Humans must change if they are to respond effectively to the challenges the world poses. If they do not change, stagnation occurs. As parents, we must try to recognize and understand the particular challenges modernity poses for adolescents. This is one of the greatest challenges we face, for we would like things to remain the same. Just think how difficult it is when we have to move to another city or adapt to a new boss and do things the way he or she wants it done instead of in a way we think is better.

Human beings are inherently resistant to change. However, the reality is that our lives are constantly changing and we have to deal with this on a daily basis. Sometimes we get angry and take our anger out on our kids because we are upset, thus decreasing our capacity to tolerate their behavior. We need to find different ways to channel our frustration and anger. This can be done in many ways; exercising, taking walks, planning pleasurable and fun activities, or adopting a hobby helps. It is important—both for our sake and our children's—to schedule free time for enjoyment and personal activities. We will be doing our children a favor if we reorganize our own lives and schedule time so we can engage in and enjoy pleasurable activities. If we make time for ourselves, we will not only be less frustrated, and happier, but we will also be better parents as a result.

Plan your future and do not revolve your life exclusively around your children. Remember they will soon be leaving for college, marriage, or work, or all three. You have your own life to live and you need to make your own plans to be happy when your children move out of the house. Many parents make the mistake of investing all their energies in the lives of their children, only to find themselves lonely and depressed when their children leave. Remember that someday, one way or another, your children most likely will leave. You therefore need to plan ahead by restructuring your life and goals so you can be happy and enjoy life without them. Think and plan for your future as well as theirs.

Do not expect your children to do with their lives what you want them to do. Your job is to teach them their options in life and help them understand the different outcomes and consequences of their choices—

such as going to college, getting a job, and entering into marriage. If you impose what you believe is best, chances are high that neither you nor your child will feel fulfilled. Adolescence is, after all, a stage of natural experimentation and rebelliousness for your children. It is during this period that they begin to design their "own way" through life in a way they believe is best for them. In doing this, they will likely take a path different from yours and different from what you might prefer for them.

In order to help your child make healthy choices, it is crucial to establish a rapport and loving relationship with your child *before* these difficult adolescent years. If you have understood and followed the advice outlined in the prior chapter for ages zero to twelve, then, when your child enters adolescence, you will have won the respect of your child. The relationship and the love you both need to continue communicating already will be set and established.

Early Adolescence (Ages Thirteen–Fifteen)

This period marks the beginning of what are commonly referred to as "the teenage years." Since the child's brain is now more developed, you are able to reason and explain to your child why certain things need to be done and how to accomplish these goals. There is some debate over how much of a directive role you should play, especially in the beginning, because the child needs to become increasingly more self-sufficient and more independent as he or she acquires more responsibility.

There are also increasing outside pressures on children from friends and peers. This is why a pattern of open communication and trust with your children is so important. You now need to engage your children in conversations more often in order to explain to them what becoming an adult means. Also, be available to talk to them when they have a problem in school or with friends. Help them understand human behavior, friends, relationships, and what life is really like. Let them know you are always there whenever they need to "talk about something that happened." Develop your children's trust by making it "safe" to talk to you about sensitive matters so they are not afraid to reach out and talk to you.

Again, remember that society changes and life is not "just like the way it was" when you were a teenager. Keep this in mind when making rules in the house, assigning chores and curfew times, etc. For example, when making rules for behavior in the house, discuss them with your spouse and include your children. Have a discussion as to why things are being done the way they are, and get everyone's input. If your children understand the reasoning behind the rules, they are more likely to comply.

During this period the most effective form of punishment is probably going to be "grounding," taking away the child's right to leave home freely. As mentioned earlier, the use of grounding must be sensitively applied and should not be for long periods of time. If it is for too long a period, the child does not see the light at the end of the tunnel and acts out or simply leaves the house on his or her own. This makes you angry, and you then have to add more "grounding" time or take the child's phone or television privileges away (each of which is also an appropriate form of punishment for this age group, though, again, not for a long period of time).

Defiance in the face of unreasonably long "grounding" punishment takes you and your child further away from a close relationship, and you risk creating an angry, vicious cycle of punishment, defiance, harsher punishment, more determined defiance—a cycle that must be broken if communication between you and your teenager is to be maintained. If this kind of cycle is generated and not interrupted during these years, the child begins to drift away from home emotionally and may even begin to demonstrate defiance by getting into trouble through more severe and detrimental associations and activities such as involvement in gangs and drugs. Such a child may well get into trouble with the law as he or she grows older.

To help prevent this vicious cycle from asserting itself, do not ground your child or take privileges away for periods as long as a month, or even a week. Instead, ground your child for a day and never more than a weekend, depending on what happened. Never cancel a birthday party, a prom, or a significant life event for the child. You may take away either phone privileges or TV for a day, or up to a full week, depending on the severity of the behavior leading to the punishment—but never both the telephone and the TV.

Remember, administer only one punishment at a time, and make it of reasonable duration for the child (to endure) and for you so that you will be able to enforce it. (Some parents feel bad after grounding their child for a month and removing the punishment early.) Remember, you must always keep your word about threatened punishment, or the punishment becomes ineffective. You and your spouse must agree, and you must back each other up. You have to have the same set of rules and remain on the same page; otherwise, the child will pick up on the division and make use of it in an attempt to get his or her way.

CASE #9

Madeline, a pretty thirteen-year-old with light brown hair and eyes, was brought to my office by her foster mother, Mrs. Morse. Madeline, along with her seven-year-old brother, had been living with Mrs. Morse for five months. Madeline's parents were divorced when she was five years old. Her father had since moved to California and had minimal contact with her for the past eight years.

Madeline remembered her father being "all right" and not abusive, though somewhat distant. Of her biological mother, Madeline said she was the "best mother in the whole world." She worked very hard, especially after her divorce, and raised Madeline and her brother by herself. Her mother's family was from Ohio and they never kept in close contact with her. Her mother was very good to Madeline and to Madeline's little brother. She was calm and spoke with a soft voice; and even though she had little time when she was not working, she managed to hug and kiss them every night and tell them how much she loved them. Madeline did not remember her mother ever hitting her.

Madeline's mother, however, had been suffering from breast cancer for three years. At first she had surgery and chemotherapy, but then the cancer spread and was now disseminated throughout her body. She was terminally ill and had been in a nursing home for several months. Madeline was able to help her mother in the beginning and did so until she went to live with Mrs. Morse. She did not want to leave her mother in the nursing home, but she had to go to school and care for her brother, who did not fully understand the concept of his mother's impending death. Madeline was very upset that she could not be with her mother. She visited her with her brother only on weekends. It was very difficult for her to see her mother deteriorate. During their more recent visits, the children's mother spoke only minimally and spent a great deal of the time sleeping.

Previously Madeline had been a good student and had never had behavior problems in school. However, Mrs. Morse brought her to see me because recently Madeline's teachers were reporting increasingly defiant behavior, angry outbursts, and frequent crying episodes at school. Madeline also was walking out of the classroom without permission and skipping classes. Her grades had been deteriorating and had recently dropped drastically. She used to be an A student, but now she was getting Cs, Ds, and Fs. Mrs. Morse also was concerned because at home Madeline would stay in her room, cry frequently, and never want to go out with her friends. In addition, she was not sleeping well at night.

When I spoke to Madeline, it was evident she was severely depressed. She was very angry and said she did not know why God had to take her mother. "Why couldn't it be someone who was mean or a criminal?" she said. Her mother was still relatively young, and she had dedicated most of her life to her children. Now she was never going to have a chance to enjoy them. "It just isn't fair!" Madeline stated. Madeline did not care if she failed school. All she wanted to do was be with her mother. She was upset that she could not see her mother more often and was angry at her father for leaving her mother for another woman: "If he hadn't left, we could all be together."

I referred Madeline for therapy and put her on an antidepressant medication to help with her current symptoms and upcoming tragedy.

This case illustrates the power of love and good parenting.

Madeline was going through the process of bereavement over the inevitable loss of her mother, the only person on this earth who really loved her. The loss of a parent, particularly a good one, is a tragic event for almost anyone. However, the younger the child is, the greater the impact because children need their parents for emotional and financial support and guidance until they become financially secure and stable adults.

The impact of divorce is also demonstrated. Madeline was correct in saying that if her father had not left them, they would be together; but more importantly their father still would be there to take care of Madeline and her brother.

CASE #10

Adam, a nice-looking fifteen-year-old, blond-haired, blue-eyed adolescent, was brought in to see me by his grandmother. He was having difficulty in school. He argued with other kids and got into fights frequently. His grades were very poor—Ds and Fs. He had been suspended a week earlier for fighting. He was defiant toward his teachers and was caught skipping school. At home Adam was constantly arguing with his mother, and they were frequently getting into verbal altercations. His mother was unable to control his behavior. He had begun having problems when he was thirteen years old, but things had really worsened in the last year.

Adam lived with his mother, his grandmother, and his mother's boyfriend, who had been living in the house for a year now. His parents had divorced four years earlier, when Adam was eleven years old. At first, he would see his father on weekends, but his father later moved out of town so now Adam rarely saw him or talked to him. Adam had an older sister who was married with two children, but he was not that close to her. After the divorce, Adam and his mother moved in with his mother's parents. His grandfather died two years ago. This affected Adam a great deal. Adam was very close to his grandfather, who was a warm, loving man. Adam said he was the only person who really understood him. His grandmother, he said, was "all right," but she usually took his mother's side when Adam and his mother argued. Adam said he had never been physically abused by anyone. Occasionally his parents yelled at him and punished him, but they did nothing abusive. He said everything got really bad at home when his mother's boyfriend moved into the house about a year ago. Not only did he take her side in everything, but as Adam said, "He tries to tell me what to do." Adam added, "He is a nightmare come true. I know my mother loves me, but she completely changed after the divorce."

Adam's mother became irritable and angry at small things. Her entire personality changed. It was as if she became someone else. Then, when her own father died, Adam's mother became very depressed and began using marijuana and alcohol. Adam said, "Then she met this guy who is a real loser. I don't know what I'm going to do. My life has become impossible. Sometimes I just wish I would die!"

I do not think Adam really wanted to die or kill himself. I think his saying this was a cry for help. In a period of four years, (1) Adam's parents got a divorce, (2) he no longer saw his father, (3) his grandfather died, (4) his mother changed and began using drugs, and now, (5) there was a stranger living with him and trying to run his life. This amounted to a total of five severe stressors within a short period of time.

Adam was completely overwhelmed by these changes, and his symptoms of anger and frustration were manifested in his behavior at school and in arguments with his mother. I decided to refer him for individual and family therapy to help him understand, cope with, and ventilate his feelings. His mother also would be counseled and urged to go to parenting classes.

This case illustrates several important phenomena. First, divorce does not have to, but usually does, cause many changes—some perhaps good but most bad, especially for the children involved. Adam's mother apparently did not want the divorce, and her mental state was severely affected. This, in turn, affected her son and all those around her. Adam was close to his dad and missed him, and somehow this was lost in the divorce. Adam also lost the love of his grandfather. His mother began to use drugs, and so slowly he lost her also. All of these losses led Adam to feel angry. Clearly, Adam also was depressed, and he manifested this by fighting in school, not caring about his grades, and skipping school to "get out of this mess."

The final blow was the arrival of his mother's boyfriend. This is another frequent occurrence after a divorce. Parents have boyfriends or girlfriends and get remarried, and this has a significant impact on the children. Children typically resent anyone new in their lives. This is why, if there is a change in the domestic situation, the family should seek counseling to process thoughts and emotions, identify and process the event, and make the change smoother and less traumatic.

LATE ADOLESCENCE / ADULTHOOD (AGES SIXTEEN–EIGHTEEN)

By this time, if a parent has done most things correctly, the challenges involved in raising children are almost over. Your teenager is about to become an adult. Basically, the same rules apply as in early adolescence, but you have to give more responsibilities to your child and also allow him or her more freedom of choice. Of course your continued guidance is still very important at this point. And if you have developed a good, trusting, and loving relationship during the earlier years, your guidance will at least be considered among the many options available when your child turns eighteen. Remember, once a teenager becomes an adult (usually at age eighteen), you have no more legal control over your child's behavior. In fact, as a matter of practical fact, beyond the age of sixteen, your ability to control and dictate to your child lessens significantly.

It is during this period that parents often perceive the most problems in their relationships with their children. If they have not developed a loving and communicative relationship, their teenagers simply say "I don't have to listen to you anymore," and they are correct. If you have followed the basic guidelines in this book, however, you will not have this problem. It is never too late to start following the principles of good parenting, but obviously the younger the child when you start, the better the chance you will have at succeeding in having a healthy and happy young adult who knows what he or she wants to do and will be a successful member of adult society.

CASE #11

Rebecca, a sixteen-year-old, slightly overweight but attractive-looking adolescent with short brown hair and brown eyes, was brought to my office by her maternal aunt, Mrs. Hernandez.

Mrs. Hernandez stated that Rebecca had been breaking house rules and curfew time. She was oppositional and defiant at times, especially at home. She also had a boyfriend with whom she went out alone. In Rebecca's native country, Venezuela, girls her age are not allowed to go out with their boyfriends without a chaperone. Mrs. Hernandez was very concerned because her sister (Rebecca's mother) sent Rebecca to Miami to live with her so that she could have a better life. When Rebecca first arrived three years before, she was well behaved and well mannered; but several months later Mrs. Hernandez began to notice changes in her behavior that were not manageable. Mrs. Hernandez's mother (Rebecca's grandmother) came to live with them six months before I met Rebecca. Since then, Rebecca's behavior had drastically worsened.

I spoke privately with Rebecca, who said her aunt was "all right" and everything was fine until her grandmother arrived. Apparently Rebecca's grandmother was extremely strict and had a very strong and demanding personality. She was from the "old school." After her arrival, she immediately changed all the rules in the house. She changed Rebecca's curfew time and did not allow her to go out with her boyfriend unless someone accompanied her. If Rebecca broke any of her grandmother's rules or broke her curfew time, she would be grounded for periods as long as two or three weeks. Her grandmother also would take away Rebecca's phone and television privileges at the same time. Rebecca told me she hated her grandmother for doing this and she had no right to impose such strict rules on her granddaughter. Rebecca felt she was losing her friends and was not socializing at all. Even her boyfriend was thinking of breaking up with her. She said she felt angry, frustrated, and very sad.

Rebecca's father died when she was a baby in Venezuela. Afterward, Rebecca lived in her native country with her mother, stepfather, and two younger half siblings. Her mother remarried when Rebecca was nine years old, and she decided to send Rebecca to the US when she was thirteen. Rebecca's half brother was now six years old, and her half sister was only three. Her stepfather had treated her decently. However, while Rebecca was living with her mother in Venezuela, her mother occasionally had hit Rebecca with a belt. Sometimes she wondered if her mother really sent her away so she could have a better life in America or just to get rid of her. When she thought about this, Rebecca pushed the thought out of her head. It was very disturbing to her. She also felt sad at times because she and her mother rarely spoke on the phone, and she missed her. She also wished her dad were alive. Sometimes she felt very lonely, unloved, and unwanted.

Rebecca clearly was suffering from underlying depression due to the multiple stressors in her life. I sent her for individual psychotherapy and family therapy. Her grandmother also agreed to go for counseling.

This case illuminates several key points. First is the severe and strict parenting of her grandmother, which led to Rebecca's defiant and oppositional behavior in response. Her mother was also strict and not very demonstrative with her love toward Rebecca. Rebecca also wished she still had her father with her to love. She was lacking love and attention and suffering from emotional neglect. If not dealt with in therapy, this could lead to poor self-esteem and depressive and anxiety disorders in adulthood. Love and outward demonstrations of love are vital to the emotional development of children and adolescents. To feel neglected and unwanted in childhood is catastrophic.

CASE #12

Victor was a handsome eighteen-year-old white Latin who came to my office accompanied by his mother. She urged him to come because he had been verbalizing suicidal desires.

Victor said he had been sad since he was thirteen years old. He felt hopeless and lacked energy. He had no motivation and experienced tearful episodes. He had become more depressed within the past few months when he began experiencing conflicts with some friends. (They wanted him to sell drugs, and he refused.) Also, there were a lot of pressures at home.

His family was originally from Santo Domingo in the Dominican Republic, but Victor was born in the US. He lived with his mother, father, two older brothers, one younger brother, and two younger sisters. Approximately three years earlier, two teenage cousins from Santo Domingo came to live with them; so now ten people lived in a three-bedroom home with two bathrooms. Needless to say, it was very crowded at home and the situation was stressful. There was much yelling and arguing at home, almost daily.

Victor was in the twelfth grade and had two jobs to help support his family. He rarely went out socially and had never had a girlfriend. His older brother molested him when Victor was five years old, and they did not get along very well. His mother had always picked on him, and he was usually the one who got blamed when there was an argument, especially among his brothers.

Victor's mother insulted him and criticized him frequently. Once, his mother had even told him he "was supposed to be a girl." He never quite understood what she meant, except perhaps that since he was the third son born to her in succession, his mother would have preferred a daughter instead of another son. Perhaps subconsciously this is why she ventilated her current anger and frustrations toward him. Victor's mother essentially was unhappy in her marriage because her husband was an alcoholic who became loud, aggressive, and abusive when he drank. She was unable to leave him because of her children and her financial situation. From Victor's point of view, his father was "all right" when he was not drinking; but when he drank, he tended to hit all the kids, especially the boys, and usually with a belt.

Recently Victor had been experiencing more frequent thoughts of death, especially since he was released from jail a few months prior to our meeting. He had gotten into an argument with his older brother, and it had ended in a physical altercation. During the fight, his brother had fallen backward and hit his head and bled from his nose. Even though Victor had not started the fight, his mother had blamed him for his older brother's injury and called the police. Victor subsequently was arrested and taken to jail. He was released a few days later. Being taken to jail on his own mother's say-so was a very traumatic experience for Victor. He could not believe his mother "hated" him that much.

Victor was suffering from a major depressive disorder. I referred him for individual psychotherapy. He had many issues to deal with and resolve. I also put him on an antidepressant medication. His mother also agreed to participate in family therapy and counseling.

This case illustrates several important points. Victor was exposed to domestic violence by an alcoholic father who was emotionally unavailable to him. His mother was extremely emotionally abusive and not very caring toward Victor. He was neglected and received almost no love or nurturance from anyone in his family. He had been sexually molested by his older brother, and his home environment was complete chaos. He could not speak to his parents even if he wanted to.

Victor had endured these stressors during all his childhood and adolescent years. The traumas he had experienced directly from family members had led to poor self-esteem, anxiety, and severe depression, which included suicidal thoughts and multiple sequelae of poor social relations and impaired functioning. He wanted to die and had no idea what he was going to do with the rest of his life or how to do it even if he did know.

Victor was the end product of a childhood-long chaotic and traumatic family. He had a great deal of psychotherapy to undergo. His age and his extremely sensitive nature presented a significant drawback. He was eighteen years old and by now should have known what he was going to do in life. Instead, he knew only that he felt miserable.

Medication and psychotherapy, though coming very late in his process of formation, will no doubt help Victor. The question is: to what degree?

Parenting Principles to Remember:

› Be available and willing to talk to your children about anything.
› Seek your children's input on decisions that affect them.
› Be reasonable and not excessive in grounding a child.
› Always keep your word about threatened punishment.

Chapter 4

CONSEQUENCES OF NOT PRACTICING APPROPRIATE PARENTING SKILLS

A s time passes and adolescents approach adulthood, they take on more responsibilities and are forced to deal with more and more high-pressure situations. They may attend college or decide to work or do both. They will meet new friends and (we hope) establish meaningful relationships with others. They may get married and begin having their own children. All these steps can be challenging, and good coping skills and emotional stability are key factors in helping young adults meet the challenges and resolve whatever problems they may pose. However, if we do not successfully provide our children with a solid emotional basis and the tools they need to cope with the inevitable difficulties of adult life, the challenges and problems will become nearly insurmountable.

Very few of us (if any) are blessed with a completely smooth and easy life, free from conflict; and as we all know, things can always get worse. We have to be prepared and ready for whatever life throws our way. Whether we lose our jobs, get divorces, become ill, or become the involuntary caretakers for loved ones who are ill, the qualities of strength and resilience are our only ultimate resources to help us solve these problems and get through the difficult times. The cases presented

THE ART OF BEING A GOOD PARENT

in this chapter will describe the most common emotional problems our children will almost certainly face if we do not follow some basic and standard rules when raising them.

CASE #13

Melissa was a pretty, well-dressed, forty-five-year-old Latin woman with brown hair and hazel eyes. She came to my office with an initial complaint of feeling depressed. She was approximately five feet six inches tall and weighed 150 pounds. Her face had a sad expression and she appeared anxious at times.

Melissa reported that she had been feeling depressed on and off for many years but her symptoms had gotten noticeably worse during the past couple of years. She had seen a therapist for several months and was taking medication, but lately she had discontinued it. When I saw her, she was crying frequently and felt very sad. She was plagued with feelings of worthlessness, low motivation, and low energy. At times Melissa even wished she were dead. She said she became easily irritated at things she later felt were insignificant. In the past she had successfully quit smoking but she had resumed recently. She was a legal secretary but was unable to focus on her tasks at times, as her mind would wander off. She had had several conversations with her boss about her declining performance and believed her job was on the line. Melissa was oversleeping and had difficulty getting out of bed in the morning. Her sleep was restless with frequent scary nightmares.

Melissa currently was involved in a four-year relationship with a man who had cheated on her and lied to her. She wanted to leave him but said it was very difficult for her. She had always had problems with relationships. She was first married at the age of nineteen, and the marriage lasted five years. She had a son from that marriage who was now twenty-five years old and married. Melissa remarried at the age of thirty, but after seven years her second husband left her for another woman. She had had other relationships, but none of them turned out successfully. At the beginning of most of her relationships, everything appeared to be wonderful, but then the romance seemed to fizzle out and she really could not figure out why.

Later Melissa began telling me about her childhood. Her parents were divorced when she was a baby, and she had no recollection of having ever met her biological father. She was raised by her maternal grandmother until the age of five, at which time her mother remarried. By the time of this second marriage, her mother had had another daughter three years younger than Melissa and a son four years younger. Her mother and stepfather came to the US from Mexico when Melissa was eight years old. They brought the two younger children with them when they migrated, but left Melissa with her grandmother back in Mexico. They brought Melissa to the US four years later. During the four years on her own in Mexico, Melissa's uncle molested her on and off for two years when her grandmother was not around. He would fondle Melissa and make her do things to him. She never said anything because he threatened to beat her up so badly she would wish she were never born. She remembered being very afraid and nervous every time he came over to Melissa's house. She would shake and tremble when she was alone with him, and he slapped and hit her if she cried.

Melissa was relieved when her mother finally brought her to live with the rest of the family in America. After not seeing her family for four years, however, it was difficult adjusting to her new life. She had to learn English and get to know her family again. At first she felt strange. Many things had happened to everyone in the family over those four years of separation, and her younger half brother and sister barely recognized her. Her stepfather seemed like a stranger. In fact, Melissa had hardly gotten to know him prior to the separation, so he also felt distant.

The most affectionate member of the family toward her was her mother. But Melissa resented the fact that her mother had left her behind in Mexico. She always thought her mother loved her the least of her three children. Melissa also blamed her mother for everything that had happened to her while she was in Mexico, including the horrible sexual abuse she endured at the hands of her uncle. When she told her mother about the abuse, her mother refused to believe her and never said or did anything about it. This further damaged and distanced their relationship.

Melissa noticed a lot of friction between her mother and stepfather. They argued frequently. Both worked long hours, and the high-pressure lifestyle in the US was much different from that in Mexico. "I don't think anyone could have imagined how different everything would be," she commented. There was very little time for the family to be together, and everyone seemed to have his or her own schedule. She also found herself taking on more responsibility for her siblings, as she was the oldest. Her parents often put her in charge while they went out.

Eventually Melissa's stepfather left the house. The fighting between her mother and stepfather had increased to an intolerable level, and they were verbally abusive toward each other almost daily. At one point her mother blamed Melissa for the problems between her and her husband, saying her stepfather had always intended to leave Melissa permanently behind in Mexico and she, Melissa's mother, was the one who had insisted on bringing her to the US. Her mother later apologized, but somehow the accusation left Melissa with a durable sense of guilt about her own role in the deterioration of the relationship between her mother and stepfather.

And then, as bad as things already seemed, they began to grow worse. Melissa's mother began to work two jobs and Melissa was left with more responsibility than ever. Finally, Melissa married for the first time. Melissa's life had never really been happy other than the few years between her marriages and other intimate relationships.

During her therapy sessions, it became clear that many of Melissa's issues revolved around her poor self-esteem. The feelings resulting from being left behind at the age of eight were overwhelming. Though her mother said she had left Melissa behind only because she was the oldest and the younger children required more of their mother's attention, it did not seem to matter to Melissa. At that age, as I have stated in earlier chapters, children think on a concrete, emotional level and are unable to reason like adults. Being left behind is equated with not being loved; not being loved leads to the conclusion that you must not deserve to be loved; and not deserving to be loved eventually translates to a lack of self-worth and poor self-esteem.

Melissa's lack of self-esteem was confirmed and deepened in her mind at the age of twelve, when her mother did not believe her reports of being sexually abused by her uncle. Melissa also felt guilty, because she thought she had helped cause her mother's marriage to fail by becoming a source of conflict between her mother and stepfather.

Perhaps the most difficult challenge in Melissa's therapy derived from the sexual abuse she had suffered at the hands of her uncle in Mexico. This severely affected her feelings of self-worth. She felt used and worthless and developed a lack of trust in men. During the sessions, it became clear her problems with relationships were connected to this abuse. Melissa tended to choose abusive relationships for herself thereafter, and her guilt from her childhood experiences prevented her from leaving these bad relationships until she "just couldn't take it anymore."

It is very common for victims of sexual abuse to feel guilt because they "allowed it to happen," even though they were children at the time, may well have been threatened, and never really had a choice in the matter.

Many think their abuse in some way was their fault and that somehow they could and should have put a stop to it. Melissa's lack of trust in men also was connected to the fact that her biological father never tried to see her, and that her relationship with her stepfather was horrible.

After several years in therapy, along with medication, Melissa's initial depressive and anxiety symptoms improved. During her sessions with me, her self-esteem also eventually began to show improvement. Her sixty-four-year-old mother was cooperative and participated in several sessions, providing a helpful, corrective experience for her. Melissa was feeling better about herself. She came to terms with and understood her past and present. She left her most recent abusive relationship, met someone else, and felt much more comfortable and at ease being with men. Melissa felt a sense of well-being and, finally, had a true chance at happiness.

This case offers an excellent example of how childhood events can affect self-esteem. The mother's abandonment and later neglect of Melissa was most prominent here, along with paternal abandonment and sexual abuse. The mother loved her daughter but did not grasp the effect her actions would have on her daughter's psychological makeup and ultimately on her life. As a child, Melissa was rarely hugged, kissed, held, or told that she was loved. She was not acknowledged in a positive manner at all. This was bad enough, but to make matters worse, she was also put down, abused, and rejected. This led to depression, feelings of conflict and confusion, and an unhappy life prior to seeking therapy.

Melissa came back to say hello several years after her therapy had been completed. She was employed in a good job and was engaged to a nice man. After many trials and tribulations, she was finally turning her life around and able to experience happiness. Sadly, there are many people who live their lives depressed because of their lack of awareness and insight about their illness. Many do not even realize the cause of their depression or have the opportunity to work through the problem with the help of a trained professional.

CASE #14

Sofia, a beautiful, slender, blond thirty-three-year old, came to my office in a severely depressed state. Sofia looked very sad, with circles under her eyes. She was well-dressed, wearing a short leather skirt, low-cut top, and a black leather jacket and boots. She also wore expensive jewelry and accessories. She informed me she had left her husband about one month earlier and was living with a friend. She was not sleeping or eating and had lost ten pounds since leaving her husband. She remained inside her friend's home almost all the time and stayed in bed a lot. She did not feel like going out or doing much. She said she had thoughts of wanting to die but would not do anything to physically harm herself. She wondered what it would be like to have no problems and be able to just go to sleep. Sofia would cry at times, but she was usually able to control herself. Her memory had deteriorated and she was not focusing well. She had not worked for several months. Sofia already had been seeing a therapist but felt it was not helping her, so she came to see me.

Sofia had been married to her husband, Mr. Carlyle, for seven years. In the beginning they were in love, but they slowly drifted apart, even though Sofia felt they still loved each other. They each had different schedules and rarely spent time together. He was a movie producer and she was a model. They had met in Los Angeles and later moved to Miami where they had lived together until their recent separation. Sofia knew her husband had cheated off and on throughout their marriage, but when she came home one day and found him in their bed with another woman, she decided to walk out. Her husband wanted her to come back home but Sofia was unsure of what she wanted to do.

Sofia's husband was very wealthy, and although she did not make as much money as he did, she came from a very wealthy family. Sofia grew up in Boston with two older sisters and two younger brothers. Her parents both came from large, wealthy families. Sofia remembered very lavish parties, weddings, and holidays during her childhood years. Her family lived in a large, estate-type home with beautiful gardens. It was a two-story home located on a hill overlooking the bay. She remembered her mother always being beautifully and impeccably dressed and her father wearing a suit to dinner every night. Her family had numerous servants, and every event was formal. Her mother almost always bought the clothes for Sofia and her sisters. All this opulent past now seemed like a fairy tale to her.

While she was growing up, Sofia's parents attended many social functions, and she and her siblings frequently remained under the care of their nanny at home. In fact, she had several nannies as she grew up, some nicer than others. When her parents were with her, they were warm and loving, especially on Sunday, which was considered family day. Her brothers and sisters all got along well, with just the occasional spats that are normal among siblings. During many summers when Sofia was young, her parents would travel to Europe and leave the children under the care of their grandparents, who did not live far away. Her childhood appeared to be uneventful and idyllic as far as she remembered. The only thing that seemed strange was that she did not like her grandfather, but at first she could not say why.

During her adolescent years, Sofia decided she wanted to be a model. She was tall and thin, and everyone told her how beautiful she was. In fact, she won several beauty contests. Her aunt frequently told her she was the prettiest of all the girls in the family. Her two older sisters also were pretty, but they were more scholarly and ended up going to Ivy League schools. One became an attorney and the other a teacher. Her brothers ended up handling the family business.

Sofia successfully completed college and received a bachelor of arts degree in history. She then went to modeling school and became a successful model, later working in California where she met her husband and was married. She never had children because of her career, but frequently she wondered if she should; after all, money was not an issue. The subject of children came up frequently in her marriage. Sofia's husband wanted children, but these discussions often ended up in arguments that left her crying, sad, and often very anxious. She frequently became depressed for several days for no obvious reason.

After her first visit, Sofia continued to come to me for therapy on a weekly basis. She recalled being sad at times during her adolescent years, but she did not seem to understand why. For no apparent reason she would stay home all weekend during those years and not go out with friends. Eventually these episodes of depressed behavior became more frequent and lasted longer. They continued on and off throughout her life, and she had gone to counseling in the past. The most vivid thing Sofia could remember was her recurrent nightmares, always involving themes of death and people or monsters trying to harm or kill her. Frequently, when she was younger, she would wake up in a sweat. Now the dreams had lessened in intensity and frequency, but her depressive episodes had worsened, especially after she left her husband. Her husband continued to call her, but she was too hurt and angry to talk to him, so she continued to live with her friend. Eventually Sofia was able to talk to her husband. I recommended that she postpone filing for divorce until she could think more clearly. It was obvious she had ambivalent feelings toward her husband and that her husband, despite his cheating behavior, loved her very much.

During subsequent sessions, we discussed Sofia's marriage at greater length. She said she had a fear of intimacy. It took her a long time to actually have sexual relations with her husband, and it was very difficult for her to experience pleasure. There was something about sex that made Sofia feel uncomfortable and anxious. Sometimes she did not feel like being touched, and she pushed her husband aside. As time passed, they seemed to have intimate relations less frequently. They would still hug and kiss, but often it went no farther.

Sofia thought nothing of the lack of sexual intimacy in her marriage until, a few years into it, she noticed her husband would go on business trips more frequently and he often stayed late at work. Before long he seemed uninterested in sex with her anymore. There were other signs that made her suspicious of extramarital affairs, such as strange phone calls and recurring, unfamiliar numbers on their phone bill, matches from unfamiliar restaurants, and lipstick marks on his shirts. He seemed to act cold and aloof at times. A friend of hers once told her that if her husband wasn't having sexual relations with her, he was probably having them elsewhere.

Sometimes Sofia blamed herself for her sexual coldness toward her husband, but why didn't he say something to her? This was when she went for counseling. Her suspicions—and her worst fears—were finally confirmed when she found him in bed with another woman.

During her sessions with me, Sofia was able to ventilate many of her feelings and pent-up emotions. She said she had begun to have more vivid dreams and would often wake up frightened and in a cold sweat. She remembered that her dreams were very scary, but she could not really remember anything specific about them. Everything seemed blurred and foggy. During one of our sessions, she had a flashback of her grandfather, who appeared somewhat angry. The picture was blurry, however, and she could not remember anything else. This happened a few more times and the intensity increased.

A few days after one of my sessions with Sofia, she called me, crying hysterically and screaming, almost in a state of panic. Her husband got on the phone and told me she had called him after attempting to slash her wrists. It was only a suicidal gesture and she was not bleeding. I told him to bring Sofia to my office immediately. She came in crying, severely depressed, and with active suicidal thoughts. I hospitalized her that day and placed her on sedative medications along with an antidepressant.

Sofia told me she had had a very vivid memory of her grandfather sexually abusing her when she was a little girl. She said that no matter how hard she tried, this memory kept coming to her mind, and she could not erase it or push it away. She also could not believe it. After a five-day hospital stay and intensive treatment with medication, she was released. She followed up with me for intensive treatment with medication and psychotherapy weekly.

Sofia's parents came in during several of her sessions, and she was able to verbalize to them her feelings of disbelief and anger. "How could my grandfather do that to me?" she asked. Her grandfather was now deceased, but she displaced her anger toward him onto her parents, who, though in a state of disbelief themselves, knew their daughter was not lying. They were very understanding about her anger and sadness.

As our sessions continued, Sofia began to understand why she did not want children and why she was afraid of intimacy. The frightening, scary thoughts of her childhood trauma had been so painful she had pushed them back, repressing them into the depths of her subconscious. But, as frequently happens, repression can go only so far. It is a defense mechanism to help us cope with trauma and the stresses in our lives. Eventually, as we get older, our defense mechanisms are overloaded, and a breakthrough of symptoms may occur, particularly when a symbolic event related to a trauma serves to trigger them.

Intimacy was a trigger for the ugly moments from Sofia's past. Once she realized what the source of her suffering really was, her relationship with her husband began to improve and they were reunited. He had come to several sessions, which was very helpful for both of them. She was still young enough to have children, but she needed more time to think about it. I slowly reduced her medication and one year after her hospitalization she was completely off the medication and feeling much better. She was sleeping better and enjoying life more, feeling more content and happy.

Sofia's case is much more common than we would like to think. Recently, with increased awareness through our schools and the media, sexual and physical abuse of our children is on the decline, although much more effort, time, and money are needed for education and prevention. Our progress against emotional abuse and its detection lags behind, as it is a less tangible type of abuse and not as easily detected.

This case illustrates the consequences of sexual abuse in children, especially girls, where it most commonly occurs. Abusive older men seem to think little girls do not realize what they are doing to them. These men do not think they are hurting the girls in any lasting, physical way and consequently convince themselves that having sex with them is "okay." As we have seen, events occurring in childhood are deeply ingrained and affect children's development. This makes it difficult to treat and eradicate the resulting problems. As we see in the case of Sofia, sexual abuse typically has severe consequences for a child. Victims of childhood sexual abuse tend to have problems with relationships and issues with intimacy. This leads to depression and affects their ability to carry out routine activities of daily living.

Although Sofia's marriage improved and her depression remitted, she was still not sure she wanted children. "Why have children just for them to suffer the way I did?" she wondered. Many who were abused as children postpone having children themselves, and some never do, not really knowing why. If she had never been abused, Sofia likely would not have been conflicted about this issue, and life would have been much simpler and happier for her. There was a happy ending for

Sofia and her husband though: they had a son two years after their reconciliation.

The importance of emotional stability as we enter adulthood cannot be overestimated. As we see in Sofia's case, lack of this solid emotional foundation causes future problems in many areas of our lives.

CASE #15

His foster mother brought Sam, a tall, dark, handsome sixteen-year-old, to my office. He appeared sad and was very guarded. He said he really didn't want to be there.

Sam was defiant at home and at school, having difficulty with authority figures. He frequently instigated fights with his peers and had been stealing for the past year, and using marijuana and sometimes cocaine. Several months before seeing me for the first time, Sam had stabbed someone while he was in the process of stealing from a local grocery store. He had spent one month in a juvenile detention center and then been court-ordered to a drug treatment program. Unfortunately, the program did not help him very much.

Sam had received therapy on and off throughout his lifetime. He was now in tenth grade, but he said he probably would fail. He indicated his grades had always been poor, but during this past school year they had gotten even worse. He was sleeping too much and had difficulty getting out of bed to go to school.

Sam's foster mother told me this was his last chance to change his behavior. She said she couldn't continue having Sam in her house unless he changed. He broke curfew time frequently, and she almost never knew where he was.

Before Sam was born, his father had left home and was never seen again. Sam had been taken away from his biological mother when he was three because of neglect and abuse. One day neighbors heard a child crying and screaming in the area of Sam's house. When they investigated, they found Sam tied to a tree with a rope. He had cigarette burn marks on his body and also older bruises which were healing. The neighbors immediately called the police. Sam's mother was nowhere to be found. After getting medical attention, Sam was taken to a shelter and placed in the custody of the Department of Children and Families. He was later placed in a foster home.

Sam was very hyperactive and defiant in school. He was taking medication for his hyperactivity, was under psychiatric care, and also saw a social worker and caseworker. However, Sam's response to medication and therapeutic intervention was poor, and his behavior grew worse as he grew older. This deterioration in Sam's behavior led to multiple foster placements of short duration. The longest one had been his current placement, where he had been for two years.

Mrs. Branden and her husband, with whom Sam had been living, described themselves as good Christian people with a lot of patience. They had been foster parents for many other children who had grown up successfully and left home. Currently their only child was Sam. Mrs. Branden appeared to be very caring. She knew Sam's complete history and felt compassion toward him and really wanted to help him.

During the first few sessions with me alone, Sam was not very verbal. The expression on his face showed an underlying sadness. He rarely smiled and had a tough and somewhat angry appearance. He answered my questions with very little expression of any kind, and his of voice was monotone. Over the first few weeks of therapy, Sam slowly became a little more open. He said he never remembered being in a warm, loving environment growing up. There were usually many other children in the foster homes he had been in, and there were always strict rules; and if you did not follow the rules, you were subjected to a lot of verbal abuse and punished harshly, many times by being hit with a belt. He said this treatment made him feel angry, and he would do destructive things out of spite. Very few of his foster parents took the time to talk to him or spend time with him, yet he was supposed to follow their directions just because they wanted him to. It seemed unfair to him. He felt unwanted and unloved. His behavior at home and at school continually caused him to face new foster home placements. It seemed to be a vicious cycle.

Every change in placement seemed to get worse, Sam said. He became more angry and defiant, and his behaviors worsened. He had a feeling of being bad and worthless, thrown around like a Ping-Pong ball. No one seemed to care what happened to him, and no one showed any special interest in him. According to Sam, all he received was punishment and rejection. The more Sam's various foster environments sought to change his behavior, the worse these feelings became. He began to hate people in general and did not seem to care what happened to anyone. No one seemed to care about what happened to him, so why should he care about others?

Sam began using drugs to escape these feelings of sadness, anger, and emptiness. Eventually the drugs became a habit, and being under their influence was the only way Sam was able to relax and experience some sense of relief and happiness. His lack of money to buy things finally led him to steal. The man he had stabbed just got in the way. Luckily, Sam's victim did not die from the stab wounds inflicted on him.

Sam did not remember much about his biological mother. He did remember being tied to the tree, and he used to have nightmares about that as he grew up. I tried to help Sam ventilate his feelings of anger and hate. At one point Sam said Mrs. Branden was one of the few people who had ever shown him affection. She would speak to him and try to understand him. Sam wanted to change so that he could remain in her household, but he found it very difficult to do what Mrs. Branden asked him to do. He was not accustomed to obeying. In therapy he continued to ventilate his feelings of anger and rejection. By making him aware of his issues and that his life was headed in the wrong direction, I helped him to develop the initiative and advantage of *wanting* to become a better person.

The most difficult problem in Sam's case was that throughout his early formative years and into early adolescence, he had never received any kind of love or affection, only abuse. It was impossible, of course, to change these historical facts. The best thing that had ever happened to Sam was Mrs. Branden. Even though it was a little late, with therapy and Mrs. Branden's continued support, some change for the better seemed possible.

Unfortunately, Sam's therapy concluded after one year, due to financial inability to continue. However, even in this relatively short period of therapy, for someone as badly damaged as Sam, he began to study more, became less defiant, and significantly decreased his drug use. I suggested he go to a community mental health center to continue some form of group and individual therapy. He still had a long way to go to continue his progress and prevent a relapse into his previous ways of coping. Fortunately, Mrs. Branden decided to keep Sam as her foster son, and at least a foundation was formed from which he could continue his progress.

In Sam's case we can see clearly how the lack of affectionate parenting can have catastrophic outcomes. He lacked nurturing, love, and affection. To make matters worse, he was rejected frequently and severely abused and abandoned by his biological parents. It is no surprise that he felt empty and had no self-esteem. We see how this leads to anger and hate. Sam's case offers an excellent example of the devastating outcomes and the significant impact our actions as parents have on our children, especially during their formative years.

This case also serves to show how and why people become criminals. Sam had built up barriers to "protect" himself from being hurt. This happens in many cases of severe abuse and neglect. It is a defense mechanism of self-preservation. If Sam allowed no one into his inner life and feelings, then no one could possibly be in a position to hurt him. He was the only one who could protect himself. This is how hard-core criminals are formed if there is no intervention. They will do whatever it takes, including killing others, in order to shield and protect themselves from being hurt. There is no sense of right or wrong or a conscience. The only thing that matters is self-preservation. These people usually have sustained multiple and severe abuse and rejection; so harming others seems a "natural" thing to them.

Chapter 5

EMOTIONAL
DISORDERS

❂

E motional disorders result from genetic or environmental factors or, most often, a combination of the two.

Genetic factors are the particular character traits with which a child is born, such as temperament, sensitivity, and intelligence. The way a child responds to situations, and the way in which these situations affect the child, depends largely upon inborn character traits, birth order, and gender. This is why each child raised by the same set of parents is different. I am not referring here to genetically inherited disorders as, for example, schizophrenia and bipolar disorder. If you think your child may have one of these problems, you should most certainly seek professional help. Do not worry. You will know if your child is subject to serious disorders such as these; teachers, especially, and other professionals will help you decide if your child needs an evaluation or specialized help.

Environmental factors include everything your child experiences during the childhood and teenage years—events and relationships both inside and outside the home. Children are influenced by their teachers, their friends, and many members of their family and extended family.

BIRTH ORDER

I will briefly divert my discussion to birth order at this point, because a lot of parents do not realize the tremendous importance of this genetic factor in emotional disorders. The firstborn child usually gets the most attention simply because there are no other children in the house and there is less stress in the family when he or she is born. When the second child is born, parents usually give most of their attention and time to the new baby because newborns require so much attention and care. Typically, the older child is not able to understand this, especially if the age difference is small (even up to seven years apart).

The older child tends to conclude that he or she is being ignored because his or her parents love the baby more. (Remember that children think on an emotional and not a rational level). This is why it is so important that you help your older child become involved in what you are doing with the newborn baby. Kiss and hug your older child during this period, and reassure your child of your love. This will make it less likely your child will resent the newly arrived sibling and misbehave in order to get your attention. A fair share of your love and attention to the older child will help prevent destructive forms of sibling rivalry later on as your children grow up together. Remember, if children do not get positive attention, they will seek negative attention because any attention is better than none.

If you then decide to have a third child in a few years, the same pattern reoccurs. However, now you have a middle child who has never experienced, and will never experience, what the first child enjoyed—receiving your undivided attention and love. The new baby now seems to be getting all the attention. If you have no more children, the baby can receive enough attention and love but never as much as the oldest because you now have three children and more responsibilities and stress. Parents, of course, do not purposely make mistakes in the way they deal with the arrival of new children, but most parents do not understand the impact their actions toward their children have on each one of them.

GENDER

Now we come to the issue of the baby's gender. Many believe, understandably, that parents should be satisfied if God gives them a healthy child of either sex, but as we all know, some parents especially desire one gender or the other, or some particular combination of boys and girls. Birth order and gender are important because all humans have both a subconscious and a conscious mind. For example, if parents want at least one boy and one girl, and their three children all turn out to be boys, the youngest boy could very well be subconsciously rejected by his parents. (In fact, this appears to have happened to Victor in case #12 in chapter 3.) While the parents love the child on a conscious level, they might treat the child differently and not even be consciously aware of it. This does not always happen, but it is a possibility. Being aware of this can help parents think before reacting to a child in ways that reinforce the potential problems created by gender as well as by birth order.

DEPRESSION AND ANXIETY

The most common emotional problems that occur in adults are depression and anxiety, and a parent's actions can contribute to or discourage the development of these disorders. Parents' impact on their children's potential for these disorders varies in degree and severity, of course, depending on how artful the parents are at various ages in their children's lives. Although there are other environmental factors in a child's life, especially during the formative years (ages zero–twelve), you the parent are the main focus of your child. Until age five, children usually do not even attend school, so basically parents are the overwhelming environmental factor in almost half of the twelve formative years.

Anxiety and depression frequently coexist. This is because many of the actions that cause anxiety also cause depression. Depression can manifest itself in many ways, such as feeling sad or empty most or part of the day tearfulness, irritability, diminished interest or pleasure, changes in sleeping and eating patterns, fatigue and decreased energy, feelings of worthlessness or guilt, poor concentration and decreased ability to think, indecisiveness, recurrent thoughts of death, and suicidal thoughts or even attempts.

Anxiety may be a part of many other disorders, but essentially some of the ways in which it manifests itself are restlessness, feeling on edge, excessive worry and inability to control the levels of worrying, becoming easily fatigued, having difficulty concentrating, irritability, muscle tension, and sleep disturbances. As you can see, many of these symptoms are common to both disorders. Also, a very common childhood disorder—attention deficit hyperactivity disorder (ADHD)—has many symptoms of both anxiety and depression and may in part be due to inappropriate parenting skills.

Preventing or Minimizing Emotional Disorders

Now let us discuss things you should and should not do to prevent or minimize your child's chances of suffering from these emotional problems. We can begin with demonstrations of your love. It is not enough to love your child silently and privately; you must demonstrate it. Tell your child, "I love you." Hug and kiss your child. (Both mother and father should do this regardless of whether the child is a boy or girl.

Some fathers feel it is not appropriate to hug and kiss their sons, but this is not the case.) Let your child feel your love and affection. Again, this should always be done, but especially during the formative years. This will help lead your child to good self-esteem (to accomplish what he wants to do in life), stability (lack of which leads to anxiety and fears), strength, and confidence.

If you consistently demonstrate and express your love, when your child becomes a teenager you will have the relationship you and your child need. She or he will be more likely to listen to you and not be affected by negative outside influences and peer pressure, which become more significant during the teenage years.

I have already discussed the most common punishment methods and which of these are most effective during the different stages of a child's development. If applied correctly, these punishments will not harm your child emotionally. There are certain punishments, however, that will have the opposite effect—that is, they will be destructive to the relationship between you and your child and will harm your child's emotional health.

There are three main forms of punishment that are never a good idea: (1) Hitting your child with a belt, or even severely spanking your child; (2) screaming and yelling at your child in an uncontrolled manner or making degrading or humiliating remarks about your child; (3) throwing things and allowing yourself to get out of control. (If you are not in control, how can you expect your child to be?)

Remember that during the early, formative years, your child thinks on an emotional, not a rational, level. If you hit your child, the emotional hurt will be greater than the physical pain of the spanking. The child thinks, "Mommy is hurting me. I must be a bad person." Internalizing these emotions leads to poor self-esteem and fears, which lead to instability and insecurity. The child also will feel sad, empty, and unloved. The child will cry and begin to feel no pleasure in what he or she does. The child may lose interest in things and become withdrawn. He or she then may become irritable and feel worthless. He or she may have difficulty concentrating in school, thinking about what happens at home and worrying about his or her relationship with parents instead of paying attention to the teacher. Nightmares, restlessness, and inability to sleep well also could occur.

Yelling, screaming, and using certain punishing words such as "stupid," "lazy," or "you are no good," or profane language will be giving the child the same message and produce the same result as physically striking the child. Again, this is because assaulting words like these are internalized and become part of the child's psyche (his or her subconscious and conscious mind). Remember, your child's brain is developing, and *your* actions and words are his or her primary input. This is why these are called the *formative* years.

These damaging methods of punishment will almost surely predispose your child to depression and anxiety disorders depending on their frequency and severity and the combination in which they are used. Also, because of genetics—the traits with which a child is born—a sensitive child will be more affected than one who is not quite as sensitive.

Please remember that you and your child will both gain more, and you will be a more effective parent, through love and understanding than through anger. You will also have a more peaceful, loving, and enjoyable home environment for everyone concerned, making parenting a lot easier.

CASE #16

Ralph, a pleasant, handsome, thirty-one-year-old man, came to my office for a psychiatric evaluation. He was suffering from severe panic attacks and appeared to be very anxious and sad. He said he was always worried about everything at work. Ralph tended to be obsessive and to get angry with himself when he made mistakes. He was not sleeping well, his appetite had decreased, and he lacked motivation and interest. Ralph had had these symptoms since he was a teenager. As time went on, his symptoms grew worse, and the worse they became, the more it affected his ability to function at work.

Ralph's marriage also was getting worse. In fact, his wife had threatened him with divorce if he did not seek help. She said he created stress for everyone by constantly worrying about little things and making a big deal out of nothing because he wanted everything to be perfect all the time. At this point in his life, Ralph was in his second marriage, and he had a two-year-old son. Ralph's first marriage had lasted only two years, but he was only nineteen years old when he married the first time. He said he loved his current wife and desperately wanted to save his marriage.

Ralph grew up in the suburbs of New York City. He did not remember being physically abused as a child. His parents did not argue very much, and they appeared to have a fairly good marriage. His father was an executive for a large industrial company, which involved a great deal of traveling, and he did not spend much time at home. Ralph was rarely able to spend time with his father, although he knew his father loved him.

His mother was a housewife, and she took very good care of him and his sister. She would take them to school and always made sure their homework was done. She always had dinner on the table at 5:00 p.m. and made sure her children followed the rules and the schedule she had outlined for them. If they needed anything, she would get it for them.

As therapy progressed, however, Ralph became increasingly aware of how critical his mother was of his own actions as a child. She never seemed satisfied or accepting of what he did, finding some fault with almost everything. She told Ralph repeatedly that it was his duty to set an example for his younger sister. His mother let him know she expected him to make all As in school, and he would be punished if he brought home any Bs or Cs.

While the punishment was never physically severe and she would not yell or scream, Ralph's mother did appear very disappointed and distraught over his every failing. Ralph was sure his mother loved him, but he felt very bad about disappointing her so often. While he typically had a very good grade-point average, Ralph was never pleased unless he could be a "perfect" 4.0 student.

His mother also was very strict with both him and his sister about curfew times and whom they were going out with. She was obsessive, in fact, about meeting the parents of all their friends. This became very embarrassing at times and limited Ralph's social life growing up as a teenager. As a result, Ralph stayed home many Saturday nights. His mother would show him affection occasionally by patting him on the back, but she rarely hugged him or said, "I love you."

Ralph wanted to be a doctor and was admitted to an Ivy League school with a scholarship. He had a high IQ and good grades and did very well on his entrance examination. In college he had fairly good grades, but at times he had difficulty focusing, as his mind would wander. Many times he wondered if he really could be a doctor, and he experienced a great deal of self-doubt. Ralph spent long hours thinking about this. Sometimes he wondered if he even deserved the chance to become a doctor. His second year of college was very difficult for him. He was not sleeping well and was becoming very sad and withdrawn. This led to a drop in his grades and he eventually dropped out of college that year. He ended up being a paramedic, and to this day Ralph feels like a professional failure because he did not graduate from medical school.

As therapy continued, it became evident there was a connection between his mother's perfectionism and criticism and Ralph's own self-doubt and self-criticism. Ralph had a vision of his mother being perfect and believed he had to be perfect as well. This was confirmed subconsciously by the punishment she employed and the lack of positive reinforcement. Ralph began to understand why he was obsessed with even the smallest thing being perfect and how this was affecting his marriage. He began to understand his wife's complaints. Knowing and understanding why he had done the things he did gave him a sense of relief, and Ralph became more secure and relaxed. His behavior at home changed, and he was able to salvage his marriage.

Ralph also was able to function better at his job. Now he understood why he did not become a doctor and to this day regrets it. But he was able to accept that now he has a family to support and going to medical school at this point in his life would be a very difficult, if not an impossible, mission. His life as a whole improved. He was relieved and felt at ease at home and at work, and he was able to experience happiness. His medications for panic attacks and anxiety were discontinued six months prior to the termination of his therapy, which lasted approximately two years. I saw Ralph again a few years later, and he told me that while he had experienced minor "ups and downs," there was nothing he could not figure out and solve. He still regretted not being a doctor and fulfilling his dream, but he could now accept his past.

Ralph is a perfect illustration of why it is so important for parents to understand the importance of good parenting skills in their children's early childhood and adolescent years. The significance of showing love and being a nurturing parent is also demonstrated by Ralph's experience. Many parents do not understand why this is important, and many think that responding with love and affection will be taken as a show of weakness on their part. They believe they might be spoiling their child with "too much love." But loving your child "privately" and not demonstrating it by kissing, hugging, and affectionate words is interpreted by the child as a complete lack of love. The child does not *feel* love and as a consequence feels bad, worthless, and insecure, which leads to decreased self-esteem, insecurity, and self-doubt, which in turn leads to anxiety and depression.

As we see in Ralph's case, a child can become extremely frightened and distraught at the thought of disappointing his or her mother. The most important thing a child can have is the certain knowledge that someone very important thinks he or she can offer something meaningful and of value while on planet Earth. This feeling of being loved and accepted, no matter what, is priceless. It empowers the child with security, great self-esteem, and a feeling of being able to conquer the world. Such a child is likely to develop excellent coping skills to help him or her overcome any obstacles encountered later in life. Such a child is likely to be happy and never experience a true depressive episode in life. This feeling prevails throughout the child's life. Unfortunately, very few of our children enjoy this inexpensive yet priceless luxury.

CASE #17

Eight-year-old Luis was brought to my office. I interviewed his parents first, while he sat in the waiting area. They said Luis was doing very poorly in school and was about to fail second grade. He was defiant with his teachers, talking back to them and walking out of class without permission. He would often get out of his seat, incite his peers, and engage in frequent arguments and fights. He had been suspended from school many times for these behaviors. His teachers also said that Luis was very active and had difficulty staying in his seat and paying attention. He was unable to focus and never completed his homework. At home he was defiant, had frequent, angry outbursts, and was easily irritated. He would get into fights with his five-year-old brother and hit him. At times he had difficulty falling asleep, but he generally slept at least seven hours a night. His sleep was uneasy, though, and he would turn from side to side and occasionally wake up crying and in a sweat after a "bad dream." His parents were overwhelmed by Luis's behavior and did not know what to do. They would frequently hit him with a belt, but the more they hit him, the worse he became.

Luis had been diagnosed with ADHD in first grade and was prescribed Ritalin, a drug that usually has the effect of decreasing a child's hyperactivity while improving focus in order to help the child pay attention in class. The Ritalin regimen was designed to help Luis in his at-school behavior. He was also seen by the school counselor on a regular basis. After a year on the drug, the school authorities stopped giving Luis the Ritalin because it did not seem to be helping him at all. In fact, he was worse than ever. The school suggested he be evaluated and treated by a child psychiatrist so he could be placed in an appropriate setting, where he could take classes at his level to help him catch up academically.

After I had spoken at length with Luis's parents, I interviewed Luis. The boy was not very cooperative at first; he was quiet and withdrawn. He also looked sad. I asked him to tell me about his family, and he said his parents argued a lot, and this upset him. They also blamed him for everything that went wrong in the house. They never praised him when he did anything they told him to do. They would never say, "Thank you" (something he was always supposed to say or he was severely scolded). "I can never do anything right!" he said, shouting. It was then that he broke into tears.

Luis said that when he argued with his younger brother Timmy, his parents always blamed him. They rarely punished his brother. Timmy was, in Luis's eyes, treated as if he could do no wrong. In contrast, Luis was frequently spanked with a belt or switch cord by his father. His mother locked him in his room or took away his television privileges for long periods of time. He said he knew they loved him, but sometimes it didn't seem like it.

Luis's mother (Lee) was of Asian descent, but she had grown up in Miami. His father, Jose, was born in Cuba and came to the US in his mid-twenties with his parents and younger sister. Jose himself experienced his parents' severe methods of punishment, having frequently been hit by his parents (Luis's grandparents). He said he was trying to discipline his own son the way he was disciplined, but lately the punishments had become harsher due to the current chaos in his life. Jose was finding it very difficult to adapt to life in the US. When he left Cuba, he really had no idea how difficult it would be. Both he and his wife had to work just to barely make ends meet. Neither came from a wealthy family, and they could not count on financial help from anyone. Jose was going to school to learn about computers in the evenings and was working at a glass company during the day. His wife had finished high school and worked as a front-desk clerk in a doctor's office. They both wanted the best for their son and wanted him to go to college.

The problems they were having with Luis at school also were putting their marriage on the line. They frequently blamed each other for not doing the correct thing for Luis, and they were having many arguments. These arguments, which Luis heard, became very detrimental to Luis's emotional health. During these arguments about Luis, Luis's mother was more passive and frequently accused her husband of losing his temper quickly and becoming easily frustrated.

It was very obvious to me that both family and individual therapy were needed. The amount of medical coverage the family had, however, was not adequate for me to work on all aspects of this case. I referred Luis's parents to a parenting skills class and family therapy at their nearest community mental health center. I started Luis on medications and offered to see him on a monthly basis to monitor his medications and progress. Luis also was seeing the therapist at the community mental health center for individual therapy.

Luis responded well to the medication. He made academic progress in school, and his behavior became more manageable. I met with his parents on several occasions when they brought their son in for his medications. They said the parenting classes had helped them a great deal. They had not been aware of how they were making their child's behavior worse and how this was affecting him in school. They were very thankful for the help they had received. On one occasion his mother told me she could now see why her husband was the way he was. Jose had learned a lot from the classes and was no longer hitting Luis, but he was still short-tempered and easily angered.

Lee suggested to her husband that he seek help for his own emotional stresses, but he said there was nothing wrong with him. He never acknowledged his own needs. Apparently he had repressed them, but at least he was more loving and accepting of his son.

Although significant progress was made, more could have been done for Luis and his family. Financial limitations and different ethnic views of psychiatry placed limits on how much we could accomplish in this case. Luis eventually made it to high school with a marginal 2.5 grade-point average. He was sociable and had friends. He said his parents still argued but less frequently. He also said he was getting along much better with his parents, especially his father. His mother had never been much of a problem for him.

Over the years that I saw Luis, I changed his medications on occasion, especially in high school when some of his underlying depressive symptoms resurfaced. His family all stopped going for counseling after several years and went only on and off thereafter.

I last saw Luis when he was in twelfth grade. He had a C average in school. He had difficulty in some subjects but was performing adequately overall. He said he wanted to go to college but was not sure of what he wanted to become. He had stopped the medication approximately two years earlier and was feeling well. He had friends and was socializing.

This case illustrates the importance of many factors, some of which we have already discussed.

Punishment methods in different cultural groups are passed on from generation to generation and affect the children in different ways, depending on their circumstances. In this case, cultural adaptation and financial stress were affecting Luis's parents and causing them great distress. Their anger and frustration were passed on to Luis in the form of severe punishment. Families under financial and marital stress have difficulty with their coping skills, and this includes their parenting skills. Children need attention and love. We have to be financially and emotionally ready to become parents, or our children tend to become yet another stressor to deal with in life. A child is far from a simple machine we can turn on and off when we wish. A child is a human being with needs that must be met one way or another.

Luis's outcome is still not known. He had a high IQ and a C average. It would be interesting to know just how far he went in college and what he eventually became. If he had come from a wealthy family, he would have received more intensive therapy than he received; but at least with intervention his parents' physical abuse was stopped and corrective measures were taken to give him a fighting chance.

Luis's defiance and anger were manifestations of his underlying depression, a consequence of the abuse he was experiencing. The lack of demonstrated parental love and nurturance undermined his sense of worth and self-esteem. Before he came to see me, Luis was diagnosed with ADHD. Many times, however, a diagnosis of ADHD is made without exploring other factors that are contributing to the symptoms. These other factors, if resolved, can lessen or abolish the symptoms associated with ADHD, which is a complex and multifaceted diagnosis.

CASE #18

Michelle, a twenty-eight-year-old, nicely dressed married woman, came to my office suffering from severe depression and anxiety. She was slim and petite, with a light complexion, short brown hair, and brown eyes. She said she was not sleeping well. It was difficult for her to fall asleep, and she woke very easily. She had frequent crying episodes and at times felt as if life were not worth living. Michelle had tried to commit suicide at the age of twelve after her parents' divorce, and had suffered from depression on and off since early adolescence. Her symptoms were now getting worse. She did not want to socialize; all she wanted to do was stay home in bed on the weekends. She was a schoolteacher and she found herself having very little patience with her students. She had become short-tempered, despite her attempts to control herself, and was easily irritated by the smallest things her students did. She couldn't wait until the day was over, and she had no energy when she came home at night.

When she first came to see me, Michelle had been married to her present husband for five years. She had an eleven-year-old son from her first marriage and a three-year-old daughter with her current husband. Their marriage, she believed, was a good one. Her husband was helpful with the children and with chores in the house. He was a good man, and they had rarely argued previously. Recently, however, they had started arguing because he had lost his job and had resumed drinking almost every day. He was a recovering alcoholic and had previously remained sober for six years. Michelle was very concerned about her husband's resumption of drinking because her first husband also was an alcoholic. He was very abusive when he drank and she eventually left him. She did not want this to happen again.

Michelle remembered her parents arguing frequently during her childhood, and her father sometimes became physically abusive toward her mother. She remembered these fights upsetting her, and afterward she would become very sad and wonder what would become of her if her mother and father divorced. She loved both her parents and they were both good to her. They loved her a lot, and when she was a little girl, Michelle could not understand why they fought. She was an only child, and this made things difficult for her. She felt lonely many times.

Michelle was crushed when her parents finally did get a divorce. Michelle was twelve years old at the time, and she felt her life had fallen apart. One night she took some aspirin, trying to get rid of her headache but not really caring if she took "too many." Afterward, she felt bad and told her mother what she had done. Her mother called an ambulance and Michelle was taken to the nearest hospital, where her stomach was pumped. She was released the following day. She said she really didn't want to die; she was just fed up with her life. After the divorce, she lived with her mother, but her father came to see her often, and she alternated weekends staying with each parent. This was difficult, but eventually she became used to it. It was comforting to Michelle not to have to see them argue and fight.

One year after her parents' divorce, when Michelle was thirteen, her mother moved in with a man she had been dating for several months. Michelle remembered this man as being mean to her and constantly telling her what to do. She soon began to feel like she was the maid in the house. Her mother's boyfriend somehow managed to brainwash Michelle's mother into thinking her daughter was primarily responsible for doing chores, which included cleaning the house, cooking, and doing the laundry. Michelle's mother and her new boyfriend were always together. Her mother rarely paid attention to Michelle and became very distant and cold.

As time passed, the situation grew worse. Michelle began to escape from her home situation by going out with her friends and staying out late at night. She was home as little as possible. She had a boyfriend when she was fifteen years old. This was her first serious relationship, and she thought she was in love. Michelle's boyfriend was nice in the beginning, but then began hanging around with guys who were "doing" drugs and alcohol and partying until late at night. She and her boyfriend started seeing less and less of each other. His attitude toward her changed, and he became less loving and more demanding.

Unfortunately, Michelle found out she was pregnant when she was sixteen years old. When she told her mother, her mother became very angry. She could not understand how something like this could happen to her daughter, especially being brought up the way she was. Her mother failed to realize or acknowledge that she had been emotionally absent from her daughter's life during her early adolescent years. Michelle's mother was seldom there to guide her and spend time with her.

Michelle's mother told her she had to get married or have an abortion. Feeling rejected and unloved by her mother, she left the house and went to live with her father. Michelle married a few months later.

Michelle gave birth to her son at age seventeen. Still, she managed to finish high school and take courses to become a teacher. Her aunt helped her take care of her son while she studied and worked part time. This was a very rough period for Michelle. Her husband had not finished high school and worked in construction. After work he would hang around with his friends and drink beer. When he came home, he was exhausted and frequently fell asleep just after dinner.

There was no romance in their lives and she felt they were growing apart. If Michelle said anything to her husband about his behavior, it would generally lead to a heated fight. When he drank, he became angry and verbally abusive. Several times he came close to hitting her. When she was twenty-one years old, she finally divorced him and went to live with her aunt. She became a teacher and met her current husband, and they were married a couple years later.

During the therapeutic process, Michelle was able to analyze events in her childhood and understand how these led to her subsequent symptoms of depression and anxiety. Therapy sessions went on for one year. At first she was given medications, but these were discontinued after nine months. By this time, Michelle was already feeling much better and more relaxed. She continued to improve, and one day she told me she didn't think she needed to come to therapy anymore. I agreed, but I told her I wanted to meet with her and her husband. I had seen him before when he had accompanied Michelle to several sessions. He had found another job, returned to Alcoholics Anonymous (AA) and had not been drinking for one month. During my joint session with Michelle and her husband, it was obvious they were both doing better, and they were able to salvage their marriage.

This case illustrates how certain events that occur in our lives affect our children. Michelle was fortunate her parents did not physically abuse her. The fact that her father abused her mother, however, created a feeling of anxiety and sadness in Michelle, leading to depressive episodes. When her parents finally divorced, she became severely depressed and anxious. (Parents are our pillars of strength; they hold us together and keep us from feeling empty and falling apart.) This is the effect divorce often has on children. Moreover, in this case, Michelle had witnessed abuse being directed at her mother, and she herself had suffered emotional abuse. This aggravated the impact her parents' divorce had on her.

Another important point, demonstrated in Michelle's case, concerns how lifestyle changes that parents make affect their children. Michelle's mother no doubt loved her daughter. However, she fell in love and began to see her daughter through the eyes of her lover. She thought he was trying to teach Michelle to be responsible by assigning her all sorts of chores, and did not realize the emotional abuse she was inflicting on her daughter. She also failed to realize she was not spending time with her daughter at a very crucial age, and their relationship was falling apart. She was shocked when Michelle became pregnant, because she really did not understand her or what was happening to their relationship. Michelle felt hurt, rejected, and unloved by her mother, exacerbating her symptoms of depression and anxiety. She was overwhelmed, to say the least.

When Michelle was married for the first time, she put up with a lot of emotional abuse, just as her mother had done. (This is what she saw as a child; and since children think on a concrete, emotional level, this is how she subconsciously thought it "should" be in a marriage. In therapy, the connection was brought to a conscious level and she better understood how distorted her thinking had become because of her own upbringing.) Our children tend to copy our behaviors and repeat them later in life. This is why we have to set a good example, even if it means making adjustments and certain changes in our own lifestyles.

Chapter 6

SOCIAL IMPLICATIONS

A s we continue deeper into the new millennium, we face a changing world full of new challenges our children must face and learn to deal with. We live in an increasingly violent world where anger and hate and conflict between people and nations are daily realities.

There has been an increase in domestic violence, which powerfully affects our children and drives them from their homes. The result is increased anger and greater chances children will get involved in gangs and drug abuse. These involvements, in turn, lead to problems with the law and criminal behavior in too many cases. Instead of learning to love and get along with their fellow human beings, children who are raised poorly learn to hate and often become hardened criminals. Since most do not work, they steal to support themselves or their drug habits. Cocaine is a particularly dangerous drug, especially if mixed with other drugs, as is frequently the case. These chemicals act on the brain in such a way as to make killing, stealing, and other criminal behavior more acceptable. People under the influence of drugs are more likely to lose control of their emotions, become aggressive, and do things they normally would not do.

In less severe cases, those affected by poor parenting have difficulty finding and keeping a job due to drug use and/or angry personalities. They have difficulty getting along with coworkers and taking orders from their supervisors, which often leads to getting fired. This only inflames their anger, making things worse. Many become a burden to society through mental illness leading to disability. Many others end up in jail. Indeed, our jails are full of people who have experienced poor parenting as children. As we have seen, good parenting not only can prevent these serious antisocial behaviors and their consequences, but it also leads to less domestic violence.

All of us have had different upbringings, and most of our parents did the best they knew how. But even a few years ago, there was relatively little knowledge about the effects parents' actions and punishment methods could have on their children, even when they reached their adult years. Usually, parents punish their children in the same manner they themselves were punished as children. As we know now, hitting with a belt or cord or other objects that leave marks on a child's body is appropriately considered child abuse. However, many parents still do this as a form of punishment because it was done to them, and they do not understand the negative effects, present and future, of what they are doing.

More and more is now known about these effects, and there is increasing awareness of the basic things parents should be doing to help increase their children's chances of achieving emotional maturity during adulthood. These concepts are not always easy to understand, and change is very difficult. Humans are creatures of habit and tend to resist change, but it can be done. It is never too late. No matter what stage of development your child is in, if you begin to adopt new, effective methods of parenting, you will lessen the impact and outcome of your previous negative actions.

CASE #19

A tall, thin, well-dressed, twenty-five-year-old Latin named Carlos came to see me for severe symptoms of anxiety and overworrying. He said he was always nervous and afraid of doing things for fear they might not be done well. He was restless, on edge, and fatigued most of the time. This was affecting his work and his relationship with his girlfriend. Carlos felt depressed when he thought of the direction his life was going. He remembered being nervous since he was a child and always fearful. He would worry constantly about everything he had to do.

Carlos's symptoms had now become so severe that he decided to come to me for help. He could not stand to continue living as he was. I put him on medications and recommended individual psychotherapy, to which he agreed. The acute symptoms improved, and we were able to begin individual psychotherapy.

Carlos worked as a bank teller six days a week. He lived in a one-bedroom apartment, which he was leasing. He was trying to save money to buy a house, but it was a struggle. He was hoping to get a promotion at the bank soon. He had been involved in several relationships but had never been married. Carlos usually was the one who ended the relationship. He felt unsure of himself and very insecure. He could never be sure if this was the "right girl" for him. The girl he had now been dating for several months was very nice, but she wanted to get married and this made him very uneasy.

Carlos had received a bachelor of arts degree in social studies but never went farther in school. At times he thought he wanted to pursue a master's in business administration, but financially it was very difficult because he would have to work full time and go to school part time. He thought this would take too long, and he was getting older and wanted to have a family someday.

Carlos grew up in Miami. His father was born in Cuba and his mother in Venezuela. His parents met in Miami. Carlos had a younger sister who was fifteen years old, and a brother who was twelve. His parents were warm, loving, and not abusive toward him. They had a good marriage and barely argued. Carlos's father was a CPA, and his mother did not work while he was growing up. However, his mother was overprotective of Carlos when he was a child. She told him every single day to be careful when he crossed the street and to be sure to look in both directions. She also told him not to talk to strangers or go home with his friends after school. She was very punctual and was always there when the bell rang to pick him up. She took him to school in the morning and went inside and left him in front of the door to his classroom. This went on until the sixth grade.

Carlos's mother kept the house spotless. Carlos said he could literally eat off the floor. Every day, she mopped the floor and cleaned the house from top to bottom, especially the bathrooms and kitchen. She washed his clothes, and his drawers were perfectly organized. You could smell the bleach on the towels. She told him to use one towel daily for his hair and another one for his body. He never used the same towel twice. When Carlos was younger, his mother would bathe him. The baths lasted half an hour. She said germs caused many diseases and she had to make sure he was completely clean from head to toe. As he grew older, Carlos found himself doing the same thing she did; it took him half an hour to an hour to take a bath.

As a child, Carlos was never allowed to sleep over at a friend's house. He could not go out to the movies, the mall, the park, or anywhere with his friends unless his mother dropped him off and picked him up. Eventually his friends began teasing him, and he found himself staying at home more and more. As he grew older, his parents became more lenient; but, still, curfew was at 11:00 p.m. on weekends; and during the week he was not allowed out of the house because he had to do his homework.

His parents wanted Carlos to go to college and pushed him very hard to study and get good grades. This is not always a good idea because kids frequently rebel, especially in adolescence, when they are pushed too much. It is more effective to explain the consequences of not going to college, especially the financial consequences of not receiving an education. Overall, Carlos's parents sheltered him to the point that his social life was seriously affected.

Carlos's father worked very hard. Carlos knew his father loved him, but his father was not very expressive. With regard to decisions concerning his daily life, Carlos tended to agree with whatever his mother said. She told him often how much she loved him, but she did not seem to understand him and what was going on in his life.

Carlos's mother once told him she had always wanted a son and she did not want anything bad to happen to him. As a result, she instilled in him a sense of fear, insecurity, and a lack of self-confidence. He was afraid of flying and could travel only by car or train. His mother's irrational and constant fears completely impaired his social life, including his ability to make and maintain friends. He lacked the self-confidence needed for forming stable relationships.

In the course of therapy, Carlos became aware of the connection between his childhood and his current lifestyle. He was able to ventilate his feelings of anger toward his parents, especially his mother. As time progressed, he felt better and more relaxed. He was becoming more secure in his actions and worried less about consequences. He eventually married the girlfriend he had at the time of therapy, after living with her for a year. He received the promotion in his job but did not go back to college. Overall, however, Carlos was able to feel a sense of self-worth, well-being, and happiness.

As in the other cases we have discussed, improvement was made. However, sometimes it is very difficult to change certain things. Carlos married, but he did not get his MBA, which would have made a big difference in his financial condition.

In this case we see how the *age at which certain childhood patterns are experienced* is a significant factor in later life. (Negative experiences in the early childhood years are the most difficult to correct.) We also see an example of how *birth order* has an impact on children. Carlos was the oldest child in his family and consequently received more attention than his younger siblings. He was, in fact, ten years old when his sister was born. Accordingly, for ten years he was the exclusive object of all the negative behaviors his mother exhibited, which made their impact even more severe.

We also see how the *sex* of a child can be a factor in his or her upbringing. The fact that Carlos's mother wanted a boy, and had one, reinforced her overactive maternal instincts of caring for her child. She overprotected him to the point of almost disabling him socially. Her own obsession with cleanliness, and her fears about Carlos's safety, served only to stunt her son's capacity for growth and led to the formation of serious symptoms.

It is true that Carlos's mother demonstrated her love for him and told him many times how much she loved him; and as we have seen, this is very important for the development of good *self-esteem.* However, she was overprotective and did not *listen* to or *understand* him. This, along with her own insecurities, had an impact on Carlos's childhood and adolescence which led to a poor outcome in spite of the love she showed her son. Carlos's case is an excellent example of how *multifactorial* childhood development is. It also demonstrates how difficult it is to be a *good parent* and why parenting truly is an *art*—an art that should be *mastered* by everyone planning on raising a child.

CASE #20

Jacob, a fair-skinned nineteen-year-old with brown eyes, was referred to me by the state attorney's office for an independent psychiatric evaluation while he was in jail. He had killed a man during an armed robbery of a bank carried out with his friends. At this time, he was facing a life sentence.

During the course of my evaluation, I asked Jacob to tell me his earliest memories of his childhood. He remembered being taken away from his biological parents because they were severely abusive. Jacob's father actually would urinate on Jacob when he became upset or angry with him. Jacob remembered being locked in the bathroom for hours at a time and being hit with belts and almost any object that came to hand when his parents were angry. Jacob had a younger brother, and he recalled that when the toddler cried, his parents would hit him and tell him to "shut up."

Jacob's parents fought with each other verbally and physically. Later Jacob found out they were both cocaine and alcohol abusers, especially his father. Jacob also remembered being sexually molested on and off by an older cousin; this was very vivid in his mind.

One day the neighbors called the police when they heard yelling and screaming in Jacob's house. When the police arrived, they found Jacob in the bathroom covered with feces. This was when Jacob and his brother were taken away from their parents and placed in state custody.

After living in a shelter for several months, Jacob was taken to the foster home of the Jones's, a very nice Christian family who legally adopted him when he was six years old. Jacob did not know where his younger brother ended up, for he never saw his brother again. Jacob's adoptive parents had a four-year-old biological daughter and desired more children, but they were unable to have them. They became interested in Jacob when they heard his story in church. However, Jacob said he was with the Jones family for only two years. They took him to a psychiatrist because they found him in the bathroom fondling their daughter. Jacob also was getting into fights at school and being very defiant at home, refusing to listen to his stepparents and getting easily angered and irritated.

After Jacob's arrival in their home, the Joneses soon noticed a change in their daughter's behavior. She became withdrawn and stayed in her room a great deal of the time. She did not eat well and would cry easily. Both children were taken for individual counseling. His stepparents' daughter improved, but Jacob's progress was very slow. The Joneses did not want to give up on Jacob, but after six months of counseling, they decided to return Jacob to the custody of the state. They did not want to risk their daughter's progress and development.

Jacob was moved in and out of several foster homes after that, each experience lasting between two and three years. He always missed Mr. and Mrs. Jones though. No other home was ever like that one. Jacob's subsequent foster parents tried to be nice and loving to him, but he did not seem to be able to respond to them. Looking back, he said his treatment at the Jones's household felt good. He wished he could have stayed there. All the other homes where he had lived had at least four children, if not more. He said he just got "shuffled around" from place to place and never felt special or wanted. He was just one of the kids. He ate and slept well, but his problems in school worsened. He was skipping school and getting bad grades. His behavior seemed to get worse from home to home. He habitually disobeyed his foster parents and did what he wanted to do. This, he thought, was probably the reason he was not wanted and had to change homes so frequently.

Jacob failed eleventh and twelfth grades and never finished high school. When he was seventeen years old, Jacob ended up in a therapeutic foster home for boys after spending ten days in juvenile detention. He was court-ordered there for illicit drug use, frequent episodes of running away, and getting into trouble with the law.

When Jacob was eighteen, he ran away from the therapeutic group home along with three of his friends. The foursome rented an efficiency apartment and split the expenses. Jacob managed to find odd jobs here and there, but basically they were minimum wage. His friends were in a similar set of circumstances. It was very difficult for them to keep up their drug habits. They stole from local stores and eventually began using knives and guns. They held up local grocery stores and small stores at shopping malls, but they never fired the guns.

Then one day one of them suggested they rob a bank. Jacob said he was reluctant at first, but eventually his friends convinced him to join them. They planned all the details carefully. One of Jacob's friends would wait outside while he and another companion would go inside and confront a bank teller. The plan was to avoid firing a gun at anyone, but just to use the weapon to create fear and compliance with their demands. However, instead of giving them the money the bank teller, an older gentleman, apparently pressed an alarm button. The alarm began to ring full blast. Amid the noise, frenzy, and confusion, Jacob and his friend were surrounded by the police. Jacob could not remember exactly what happened because everything occurred so fast, but he panicked and, in a moment of despair, shot the elderly teller, who died on the way to the hospital. Jacob was arrested by the police, held in jail without bail, and charged with second-degree murder.

I performed a mental status examination. Jacob was not sleeping or eating well. He was very withdrawn and guarded, and his face was tense and masklike. He seldom looked me in the eyes, but when he did, his eyes had a sad look. At times when he spoke, he became loud and angry. He kept saying, "It just isn't fair," in a loud voice as he paced back and forth in his cell. His underlying depression was being manifested by loud, angry outbursts and aggressive behavior. He would throw objects against the cell walls, scream, and bang his head against the bars. He would also break down and cry, yelling, "Why? Why? Why?"

Jacob had been given a major tranquilizer, and there was a security guard constantly present with me in the cell. Somehow, though, I never felt threatened or afraid that Jacob would hurt me. He was harboring a great deal of anger, which was being ventilated the only way he knew how. He was not insane and was in touch with reality. He denied having hallucinations and he was not paranoid. I tested his cognitive functioning—that is, his ability to think, concentrate, and remember. He performed fairly well considering the circumstances.

Jacob was sorry he had killed a man, but he was not particularly remorseful. He appeared to be more concerned with his own circumstances. He could not believe his life had ended up this way. He expressed death wishes at times but denied he had any real intention of hurting himself. I diagnosed Jacob with major depression and antisocial personality disorder. I recommended that he be started on antidepressant medication. He went to trial and, after consideration of all the facts in the case, was sentenced to serve twenty-five years in prison.

Unfortunately, cases similar to this one are very common in our court system. Some involve less severe crimes, but many result in the death penalty for premeditated murder. Many offenders at this level of criminal behavior have genetic psychotic disorders or histories of multiple drug abuse which predisposes them to criminal acts, depending on other circumstances in their lives. However, it is very common to find a history of severe physical and emotional abuse in their childhood, along with dysfunctional families, parental abandonment, and the witnessing of physical abuse of other family members, including their own parents.

Children who are raised in this kind of environment typically grow up not realizing the distorted nature of their situation. They eventually reach a point where they do not think much about it at all, and in many cases they grow up thinking such an environment is normal and "okay." They were not taught anything else. When they go out into the real world, they do not know what to do and are confused as to what is wrong and what is right.

Jacob's case clearly illustrates one of the worst societal outcomes of bad parenting. The sad thing is that in most of the cases that involve serious criminal activity, change is extremely difficult at best and often nearly impossible. Jacob never received therapy. He was one of the many cases that "fall through the cracks." He was not caught in time to effect any meaningful change in his pattern of behavior.

If children and adolescents end up serving prison sentences, we have lost them. They will be much older when they get out, and therapy, if available to them, will be less effective (their personalities have formed). They generally continue to do what they were doing before going to jail. Because of this, they tend to end up in jail again. It is not unusual to see criminals returning to jail repeatedly. Building more jails clearly is not the best and ideal answer.

Chapter 7

CONCLUSION AND FINAL THOUGHTS

I hope you have found the information presented in this book helpful and informative. As I said at the outset, my goal is to help couples understand the *why* of good parenting practices and not just the *how*. With this sort of insight, you will be more capable of coming to an educated decision about whether and when to have children.

If you have been physically, emotionally, or sexually abused and feel you need help (this is very common), it is paramount that you enter therapy before you have any children. You need to be in control of your emotions so that you do not displace your anger, frustrations, and trauma onto your children. Most parents who make significant parenting mistakes (e.g., physical punishments or loud yelling and screaming at children) do so because of trauma they themselves experienced or, in some cases, because of ignorance or a lack of instruction. It is important that you not have children until you are emotionally ready to be a parent. This means finishing your preparation for a career, being in a stable relationship, and being financially stable. Certain things you want to do in your life, such as travel, should be done before you start having children.

It is crucial that you solidify your relationship with your partner before you become a parent. You need to give yourselves time to enjoy being together as a couple before having children. It is very difficult to travel and to partake of social activities and events when you have young children. The first few years of child rearing will take up a lot of your time and energy. With children you need a lot of patience. The less stress you have in your life, the easier and more enjoyable the potentially joyous experience of having a child will be.

Remember that each of us is unique and we each have our own different lifestyles and personalities (character traits). What I have tried to do is provide you with useful information to help you make more informed decisions as you raise your child. I urge you to try to adhere as best you can to the basic rules of good parenting outlined in this book. Remember that there is both love and anger. It is up to you to choose the kind of life you want for you and your children. With the right education and framework, love will win out.

We are entering a new era. Our world has new and different problems we must learn to conquer. We cannot be stagnant, for the world we live in is not. Our children and grandchildren need to be emotionally healthy and strong to successfully confront the difficult challenges they will face in an increasingly complex world. This is why it is so important that we also change to meet the challenges of our time. Important in this task is our ability to learn from all the new knowledge and scientific findings related to parenting that is available to us.

In conclusion, it is important to remember that while we might dislike and be resistant to adopting new ways of thinking and living out our lives, the world will be a better place for our children and for generations to come if we are willing to listen and learn from the voice of love and reason.

BIBLIOGRAPHY

Bowlby, John. *Childcare and the Growth of Love.* London: Penguin Books, 1953.

Bowlby, John. "The Nature of the Child's Tie to his Mother." *International Journal of Psychoanalysis* 39:350–71.

Diagnostic and Statistical Manual of Mental Disorders, 4th ed. (DSM-IV). Arlington, VA: The American Psychiatric Association, 2000.

Freedman, Alfred M., and Harold L. Kaplan, eds., *The Comprehensive Textbook of Psychiatry.* Baltimore: Williams & Wilkins, 1967.

Talbot, J; R. Hales, and Stuart C. Yudofsky, eds., *Textbook of Psychiatry.* Arlington, VA: American Psychiatric Publishers, 1988.

About the Author

Rosa F. Turner, MD, was born in Cuba and raised in the United States. She graduated from the University of Florida, obtaining a degree in chemistry and pharmacy. After serving as a pharmacist for several years, she decided to continue her education and became a medical doctor specializing in child, adolescent, and adult psychiatry. She completed her specialty at the University of Miami School of Medicine, Department of Psychiatry in 1989 and became board certified in 1990 by the American Board of Psychiatry and Neurology. She is currently a practicing psychiatrist in Miami-Dade and Broward counties in South Florida.

During her twenty-four years of private practice, Dr. Turner has held medical director positions at several hospitals and adolescent units in the South Florida area, including Harbor View Hospital, American Day Treatment Center for Adolescents, and Charter Hospital of Miami, and has served as clinical assistant professor at the University of Miami Jackson Memorial Hospital.

She has been very involved in her community in research projects and speaker programs and is highly regarded in her specialty.

Dr. Turner has devoted a large portion of her life to educating and helping others.

www.ingramcontent.com/pod-product-compliance
Lightning Source LLC
Chambersburg PA
CBHW021343090426
42742CB00008B/723